PRAISE FOR *THE CLOCK M*
NOMINATED FOR :

T.S. Eliot famously praised poets "who feel their thoughts as immediately as the odour of a rose" and until Michael Salcman our recent poetry has been overdue the new arrival of such a poet... This is a question-asking, passionately felt, superbly described and crafted poetry of the highest order.   —Dick Allen

PRAISE FOR *THE ENEMY OF GOOD IS BETTER* (2011)

Michael Salcman's poems are erudite but wear their erudition lightly. His range is enormous. No matter his subject, his poems are in love with life.   —Thomas Lux

PRAISE FOR *A PRAGUE SPRING, BEFORE & AFTER* (2016)
WINNER OF THE 2015 SINCLAIR POETRY PRIZE

A Prague Spring is a near-epic book of history poems, interweaving the story of Prague with the Holocaust, family deaths and survivals, a book that stuns the reader with the enormities and sorrows of Time.   —Dick Allen

PRAISE FOR *SHADES & GRACES: NEW POEMS* (2020)
INAUGURAL WINNER OF THE
DANIEL HOFFMAN LEGACY BOOK PRIZE

Brilliant, playful, rueful, profoundly grounded—a scholar of Erasmus and Sinatra, pinball and neurosurgery—Michael Salcman knows how tricky ideals become when you try to live them—whether you live for beauty or to repair the world or both. Salcman is a poet who has paid his dues, crafted a voice whose modulations are seamless: the profundity is natural as daylight. In *Shades & Graces*, his canvas is life's entire arc.   —D. Nurkse

NECESSARY SPEECH

New & Selected Poems

Michael Salcman

SPUYTEN DUYVIL
NEW YORK CITY

ISBN 978-1-956005-12-7
Cover: "The Wrath of Children" (2019), deconstructed cloth print portfolios on canvas,
© Samuel Levi Jones, courtesy Galerie LeLong & Co.

Library of Congress Cataloging-in-Publication Data

Names: Salcman, Michael, author.
Title: Necessary speech : new & selected poems / Michael Salcman.
Description: New York City : Spuyten Duyvil, [2022] |
Identifiers: LCCN 2021036095 | ISBN 9781956005127 (paperback)
Subjects: LCGFT: Poetry.
Classification: LCC PS3569.A45924 N43 2021 | DDC 811/.54--dc23
LC record available at https://lccn.loc.gov/2021036095

.

NECESSARY SPEECH (NEW POEMS)

I

Because   5

His Tongue   6

By the Way What Time is it in Prague, Milena?   7

The Boys in the Office   9

The Burned Field   10

Visiting My Father in His Final Illness   11

Song for Two Mothers   12

Rockefeller's Gift   14

Unreliable Narrator   15

Three Days in Germany   16

The Best We've Ever Had   18

Sake   19

Getting Older   20

Surrealism Comes with Age   21

Old Fish   22

Poem to a Cane Placed Upside Down   23

II Plague Poems & The Hours

A Poem by Dr. Rieux   27

Social Distance in the City   28

A Prayer in the Plague Year   29

Walking the Edge of Death   30

Intensive Care   31

Every Picture But One   32

No Translations for Love   33

Yesterday's News   34

The Cleft Chin   35

First We Name You   36

The Hours   37

III

White Space 51

A Memory of Málaga 52

Clement Greenberg, Living in My Head Rent Free 53

Pictures on a Trembling Wall 55

Mannequins 56

A Painting Called "Winter" 57

Correspondence: Deep Yellow—Green 58

His Name Meant Light 59

Summer Conference with D.D. 61

John Updike's Trash 62

Twelve Reflections on Francis Picabia 63

Matisse: Self-Portrait as Serf 66

Matisse: The Knife Thrower 67

Epiphany 68

The Good Tourist 69

IV

Event Horizon 73

How the Professor Rose 74

The Muscles on the Muscle Man 75

In the Morgue 76

Heard in a Museum: John Cage Sonatas 77

Baltimore's East Side 78

Blown Up 79

Blind Spot 80

Lies Before Retirement 81

Insistence 82

Reversal 83

Wounds 84

The Empty House 85

Selected Poems From The First Four Books

From The Clock Made Of Confetti (2007)

Perfect   91

Sitting Shmira   92

Fish Talks, Town Buzzes   93

A Bleak and Gaudy Carnival   95

The Clock Made of Confetti   96

Lady Heart   97

Photography: A First Course   98

In Old Barcelona   99

Dr. Williams Delivers a Baby   100

What He Must Have Been Thinking   102

September Sonnet   104

Notes on First Hearing Alkan's Funeral March   105

Notice in *The Times*   106

Be Not Afraid   107

Small Bones   108

George Stevens Makes A Movie   109

Back to the Future   110

The Unlabeled Dead   111

Katya's Great Romance   112

The Passage   114

Wrestling in Brooklyn   115

The Year the Dodgers Won the Pennant   116

This Is The Hand   117

Our Son Discovers Pantyhose   119

The Ice House   120

The New Man   121

The Block   122

The Bargello   123

Titian's Last Painting   124

The Rokeby Venus   125

Stubbs Not Seen   126

Eight Eakins Portraits: 127
       I-The Pair-Oared Shell (1872)
       II-The Gross Clinic (1875)
       III-The Swimming Hole (1883-1885)
       IV-Portrait of Walt Whitman (1887-1888)
       V-Miss Amelia van Buren (1891)
       VI-Portrait of Professor Henry A. Rowland (1897)
       VII-Portrait of Mrs. Thomas Eakins (1899)
       VIII-Self-Portrait (1902)
Gauguin's Hand   132
Looking at Kline   133
Blue: Barnett Newman's *Ulysses*, 1952   134
Double Orange Car Crash   135
Deconstructing Abstraction   136

Red: The Color That Advances   137
Love In The Age of Mechanical Reproduction   138
Missing You, I Notice Things   139
Romantic Organ   140
The Offering   141
Scent   142
Quantum Love   143
A Dream of Jaguars   144
This Is Not a Rehearsal   146

The Gray Cat   147
Magical Thinking   148
The Road to Machu Pichu   149
The Phone Call   150
Drowned River at the Lazy Moon   151
Shooting the Moon with a Sextant   153
A Lamentation of Swans   154
Language and the Brain   155

From The Enemy Of Good Is Better (2011)

Euphoria   159

When the Boy Comes Back   160

H*O*R*S*E   161

The Family Name   162

Indecent Desire   163

Clearing the Brambles   164

Cutting Apples   165

Three Deaths   166

The Doctor Gets A Daughter   167

Bitterroot   168

Everything But The Ashes   169

Sea Nettles   171

Poem on a Single Word from Richard Serra's Verb List   172

Suppose You Miss The Lightning   173

The Urge to Jump   174

The Body Painted In Grief   175

Metonymy: Part For The Whole   176

Elegy: Saul Bellow   177

Turner Sets Out in a Snowstorm   178

The Rough and The Smooth   179

The Dog Speaks   180

In the Lost Movie of Its Making, Pollock's Red Painting   181

An Uncommitted Crime   182

Contra Chekhov   183

At Green River Cemetery   184

Baltimore Was Always Blue   185

The Long-Ago Dead   186

Caesar's Last Breath   187

The Apprentice Surgeon   188

Intensive Care   189

Mother of the Bay   190

A Season Like This   192

Bird on a Wire   193

I Gave My Ticket to a Blind Man   194

Last Saturday Morning in Boulder   195

A Song of Spirals   196

Heat Lightning   198

Zamboni   199

The Enemy of Good is Better   201

Water Psalm for St. Michael's   202

Navigation   203

Scenes From A Marriage: 204

        1-Al Fresco

        2-Rt. 101 Heading South

        3-Drowsy

        4-Kiss the Coffin

        5-This Spring in Baltimore

        6-Unruly Nouns

        7-Still Pond on the Bay

        8-Rehearsing the End

Putting the Boat In   210

The Painted Nightgown   211

To the Mistress of the Master of the Female Half-Lengths   212

FROM A PRAGUE SPRING, BEFORE & AFTER (2016)

Prologue   215

"1944":   217

        1-(The Dead)

        2-(Meeting Miklos Szabo)

        3-(The Factory)

        4-(Defenestration)

        5-(In the Cellar)

        6-(The Truck)

        7-(Arnold)

        8-(Magda)

        9-(Pinkas Synagogue)

        10-(Alfred)

Questions for Kafka   227
Benjamin Thinking   228
A Picasso Portrait : Max Jacob   229
Final Villanelle   230
Veiled and Unveiled   231
Uncle Rudi by Gerhard Richter   233
Coyotes in Connecticut   234
Beating   235
The Gift That Keeps on Giving   236
Lech Lecha   237

An American Refugee on Vacation in Prague   239
What Do Little Children Know   240
At La Provence   241
Prague Suite :   242
     1-(Prague Time)
     2-(Staré Město)
     3-(The Old Jewish Cemetery)
     4-(The Golem)
     5-(Little Quarter to Kampa)
     6-(Charles Bridge)
     7-(Jan Palach)
     8-(Each Death A Wound)
Envoi: First Love   250

V—FROM SHADES & GRACES (2020)

Ten Reflections on Ramón Gómez de la Serna   253
The Three Weisses   256
The Duke of Flatbush   257
In The E.R.   258
Not All Will Heal   259
HM The Man Without A Memory   260
On The Anniversary of the Moon Landing   262
That September, You Remember 1975   263
That Stinking Rose of Garlic   264
Showing the Apartment   265

The Lost Notebook   266
Alien   267
The Old Boat   268

What's Left Out   269
The Drone   270
Quandaries and Lies   271
Medulloblastoma   272
Of Wanting There's No End   273
No Wires, No Shackles   274
Mobtown   275
Mendacity   277

from Father Sleeping   278

The Blizzard   282
When Bach Was Street   283
Graffiti   284
The Vicar   285
The Marled Beam   286
Vissi d'Arte   287
Seven or Eight Reflections on Erik Satie   288
Last Night at the Huguenot House with the Black Monks of Mississippi   291
At The Reading I Don't Mean   292
In-Painting   293
How The Trick Is Done   294
The Cult of Beauty   295
Talking to Mother & Father   296
Winter Poem   297

IN GRATITUDE   299
ACKNOWLEDGEMENTS FOR NEW POEMS   300
NOTES FOR NEW POEMS   302
AUTHOR'S NOTE ON THE TEXT   305

NECESSARY SPEECH
(NEW POEMS)

I

That's the struggle of humanity,
to recruit others to your version of what's real.
—Saul Bellow, *The Adventures of Augie March*

BECAUSE

I tell her more often now because
she is ageless and I am over seventy.

Because it's the same girl's face
I first got to know fifty years ago
with the same sunburst of energy.

Because starting out together was predictable
but the end of either one may come
like a ballooning shadow.

Because so many things people say
have indefinite meanings
but these three words are ever unambiguous.

Because I have breath enough to say them yet
and she has generously listened.

Because she is not a cat and I am not a dog.

His Tongue

My grandson yells because he cannot hear,
slowly he's learning words part by part
his father repeats over and over,
each plosive like a block thrown at a wall.
He grabs at his "super ears," first pulling them off
then putting them on when the world disappears.
Hungry for words he looks into the digital camera
and smiling says something a lot like Bubbe
or Grampie or any other word welding us
together. We strain to understand what he means,
is it love or frustration mixed with peanut butter
beneath his tongue, marinating meaning
on the mouth's grill? He builds highways
with his older brother, dances ballet with his sister,
makes some think it's not the ear but the brain.
I hope that isn't true; I've been there with scalpels
and suckers and electrodes for years:
the brain's beyond calculation, the ear just a bell
in a symphony. I kiss the screen with my lips.

By The Way What Time Is It In Prague, Milena?

It's almost always too late or too early in Kafka's writings,
like the parable in the letter he wrote his lover Milena
about two people each holding a door handle
on opposite sides of the same room, and walking out
or not, sounding a lot like Schrödinger's quantum cat
in a closed box, alive and dead at once.

No wonder it's almost always too late or early for Kafka,
Milena's own grandmother kept her clocks one hour ahead
in protest of the imperial time of Vienna
not to mention the backward-running clock
in the Jewish ghetto and the quadruple register of time
on the astronomical clock in Staré Mêsto.

When construction of St. Vitus Cathedral stopped
for 450 years it was considered only a brief interruption
of shortened time like a speeding bullet or a light ray
from Alpha Centauri. No wonder Einstein's lecture on time
took place in the same rooms where Kafka and Rilke spoke poetry,
no wonder Poincaré received honors at Charles.

Here was a city outside of ordinary time,
riding a chronological wave forward and back,
earlier and later than Paris in every way—it needed an Einstein
to teach its burghers how telling time was possible in such a city
and a Kafka to tell them time didn't matter
when life was an illusion anyway.

So it's almost always too late or early with Kafka,
those broken engagements, his midnight-blooming
passions, his day dreaming into the street
from a window in the Kinsky Palace
where he wrote above his father's store.
Too early for Kafka to see his three sisters dead

in the camps and Milena perish in the Second World War.
Way too early for Kafka to see his name painted everywhere
in the Old Town Square, on bookstores and tea cups,
on tavern walls and hotels, the twice-hated German-speaking
Jew who kept himself private even as he fled
the same cobbles and avenues many years before,

always too late and always ahead, a typical Czech.

THE BOYS IN THE OFFICE

—They Feed the Lion, Philip Levine

In those first few months after we arrive in America
my father works outdoors, labors under heavy bags
of cement, an educated man working like a mule
to support us. His servitude ends with a real job
in a company that made parts for missiles and tanks,
pin setters for bowling alleys, Roadmaster bikes.
He never actually lied but let them think he was Italian
for years: the dark complexion, the broad family nose,
the exotic accent, it all seemed a plausible disguise.
He never actually lied, laughed when the boys told jokes
and gibes, never knew if they suspected a Jew
was among them, a senior engineer like he once was
at the Škoda works before the war, before he fought
the Nazis in barns and sewers with Czech partisans,
in the secret code of the underground. He drew blueprints
in New York for the Food Service Division, perfected
machines that cradled plates in three-pronged jaws,
hot or cold. At times, he must have forgotten
where he was, afraid he might lose his job if anyone knew.
This gentlest man lived like a spy while mother and I
went to Broadway shows and concerts at Carnegie Hall.
Dressed in gray, my father signed over his patents
to the boss, got a dollar for every invention, felt safe
but cheated of his knowledge, trembling he might lose
the job that kept mother and son off the streets.

The Burned Field

Two ancient relatives, my father and newly united
cousin Carl from Sarasota
are touring sepia-toned family pictures in St. Pete.
Great grandfather Joseph, bearded in a short vest,
stares out from the photo that interests me the most,
a yarmulka on his head and farmland behind.
His wife, in peasant dress, sits pear-shaped at his side,
and two of their nine children are on his knees:
cousin Carl's mother and my father's father,
not struggling, calm
two of five siblings who perished in the war—
a connection proved here in black and white.
Four others came to America just in time, and some,
like those in Cleveland and Brooklyn, too late
brought us over after it was over.
My father and his cousin try to bring it back, the old life,
speaking of Joseph the rabbi, mortally kind,
and three score left behind in cinders.

VISITING MY FATHER IN HIS FINAL ILLNESS

South of Stamford
the island of Manhattan shims into view
like a great battleship turning,
buildings standing in ranks like turrets,
round after round of squared off cannon
and chutes and ribbons of smokeless stacks
in which millions of fires live and burn,
the island as gray as the long-lost model I made
of the war wagon *Missouri*.

Numerous trestles of small bridges pass,
the trash screes down to the edge of the track bed
in waves and on the roadway's walls,
a graffito of letters and numbers greets
our lumbering torpedo making its way
out of the city, its most desperate parts
glowing faintly in the late afternoon light:
the bricked-up hives of Co-Op City
and Riverdale's carnivorous streams.

We came as ghosts to Babylon
and depart the same, the East River beats
in our hearts, the ancient stones of its roadway
leap outside the windows of our train.
See them suddenly gone, a million man-years
at once subsumed by the earth:
the green inlets of the Sound,
the small rivers of Connecticut,
the childish boats at play in Greenwich
shivering like soldiers after a truce
surprised at life in the nearness of its enemy.

Song For Two Mothers

Miriam and her sisters sang and danced at the edge of the desert
And the sea of Galilee; it was night
And neither brother came to see the celebration.
The women clicked timbrels in their hands
And sang tributes to the moon and its divination
Of bloody power. Beneath their skirts the future oozed
Like a premonition of divinity, like prophecy.
Who were these prophets and lords of a foreign desert
Who foolishly claimed a future
And inscribed their masculine jealousy on stones?
The people drank wine and abolished the dark for a while.
Priests came with their silver adornments of primacy
And asked them to stop whirling like wind-blown grains.
Look over the mountain tops they said and gaze on the future.
But it all seemed the same like a backward tomorrow.
My mother's Hebrew name was Miriam; my father's Aaron.

At ninety-eight my step-mother Simi still walks on her treadmill
Makes banana smoothies after exercise, her numbers long-faded,
A survivor of the place too terrible to name,
Where she and the other women slept in their lager
On top of one another like cords of wood.
She was the sole entertainment,
Reciting from memory *Gone with the Wind*,
Not the screenplay but the book, eating that day's extra potato
In filthy water, the reward they gave her for keeping them sane.
The future was in America where Miriam would die too young
And after Simi lost her husband she married my father
Who survived by fighting in the underground:
He never saw the camps and had no numbers on his arm.
She made him travel and learned to play golf, and she saved him
From his sorrow. When he passed at ninety-nine

Simi nudged my shoulder at the cemetery
Whispering in my ear the optimist's credo, "You know, Michael
He never thought he would ever die."

ROCKEFELLER'S GIFT

Mother and I sit in a government office trying not to think about
the one thin dime the governor's grand dad used to give
beggars on the street. Eleven years after we come to America
I finally meet my first important black man: he's severely thin
and looks like a piccolo with a white-inflected voice,
his handshake holds no hint of promise,
even if his name sounds a lot like French money.
On the chance we get the grant, Mr. LeMonier says it must be spent
in New York…unless, and here his eyebrows raise with possibility,
there's a special course of study the Empire State doesn't have.

Mother looks too young and I'm fourteen with an ankle and calf
two-thirds gone from polio. I'm daydreaming of playing Lear
on Morningside Heights, half-attending to her next question—
she who presumes her wish is mine, as if she might be the one
doing college and medicine in Boston twelve months a year.
But each time she antes up a new exception he says "yes",
both of them watching me ignore their conversation.
At last he shakes his head in my direction before fixing his stare
on her: *And what will you do if he doesn't get the money?*

Mother blinks once or twice and gives him a glare
like Cordelia might, unclenching her mouth—*Then he'll still go,*
and I, having lost the last bit of air in my chest, watch him lean back
in his chair, pyramiding his fingers in front of his mouth,
as he lets the dime drop: *That was the right answer.*

Unreliable Narrator

In Connecticut my dead sleep along the train tracks by the highway. You can see them from your window in their ranks and rows as you pass, their headstones leaning with the discomfort of constant interruption, wheels squeezing on rails, horns blowing in warning. I once knew these towns like I knew myself, how they made New England's solemn necklace of habitation stitch across rivers and inlets, the valuable water views realtors reserve for the living. My parents in Groton are probably saying I should calm down, my father turning a knowing smile to my mother, glad they missed the change in my daughter who thinks she's writing this, just as she says she chose us as parents before she was born, insists on having telepathic connections to other great souls. She wants me to piss my pants, to settle the score. Like I said it goes back before college, before childhood, before she was born, always at war. You mustn't hate your parents, I would like to tell her, the most interesting people you will ever meet. A moment more, I pass a green pond, where three egrets stand like ghosts. The train's getting close to my destination.

THREE DAYS IN GERMANY

For Henri Poincaré art and science were much the same,
from all possible combinations we choose what to put in
and what to leave out, picking a perfect flower from a wet
bouquet. I wanted to call this report Three German Tales
but they're all one story. It was raining the second day
Professor and Madame went from Frankfurt to Heidelberg
by train, a light drizzle falling against their first class windows.
Thirty years have passed since he last came here
to teach U.S. Army doctors about the brain.
Age had converted him from one end of the bed
to the other. On the street it was difficult for his ankle
to walk the cobbles; everywhere else he looked for flat paving
stones but at the ruined castle in the side of the mountain
it was hard to step care-free. Clouds came and stayed,
the trees on the Philosopher's Walk glowed green.
Near the mouth of the courtyard a plaque he couldn't read
probably said 'here stood Goethe watching the moon dizzy
with love.' And across the broken stones the Weinstube
restaurant where once he ate wild boar from the Black Forest
covered in almonds and ox-tail soup with passion.

ii

The day before they visit the castle the Professor and his wife
went to the Städel in Frankfurt, going floor to floor, stopped dead
by an unknown Flemish Master and a Bellini Madonna painted
Venetian blue. It was his father's birthday but no longer necessary
to call. At last they stood before Tischbein's famous portrait of Goethe
reclining in the Roman *compagna* like a courtier, wearing
an enormous black hat, a pigeon-gray smock and *two* left-footed shoes.
Did his great brain forget to properly dress the morning he posed
or are true poets bent in a way only their painter can guess?

There the Professor stood dreaming of *apfel* beignets floating
in crème anglais—powdered sugar and cinnamon crisped around
the cold heart of the fruit. This fabled dessert from his last visit
thirty years ago, a treat invented in Heidelberg and unrepeated,
mourned and searched for like that cake in Combray.

iii

The day after the castle, they walk along the Hauptstrasse
to the Hotel Ritter where people claim to have invented *apfel* beignets.
No one in the Professor's family believes such a glory exists
in a country not fabled for its cuisine but Madame insists
he shall taste it again. The waiter at the Ritter speaks of change
in the kitchen: they no longer make beignets, only apple strudel.
It's as if a great tenor had left the stage. On the train back
the couple sits in a private compartment with plush velour,
particolored seats, and arm rests as thick as his thigh.
The other four places remain unoccupied. There's no service
and all the announcements are in German.
The train curves out in front of their eyes, inscribes a turn
with its great length; Madame sits as silent as Ingrid Bergman,
the Professor pretending he's a spy like Cary Grant
stares down the tracks where the gray trains still run on time.
That evening the barman at their hotel talks the chef into making them
apfel beignets. The waiter is French but dressed like a floor manager
at Fortnum & Mason. Since London he has lived in Frankfurt thirty years
but will retire to an island on the Bay of Biscay where he can fish
and drink red wine the rest of his days. The Professor takes a bite
and nods to his wife. You can imagine the taste, exactly the same.

THE BEST WE'VE EVER HAD

After a weeklong cruise from Barcelona and an intermediate stop in Marrakech, we landed in Lisbon. We encountered a lovely bidet. This was not surprising; such fixtures—more rightly a type of sink than a species of toilet—are almost universally installed in the southern European countries. They are only a little less widespread in France, where they were probably invented by furniture makers in the late seventeenth century. They are almost never seen in Northern climes. Bidet comes from a French word for pony; in Old French *bider* means "to trot" and one "rides" or straddles the bidet as one rides a small horse. This history inevitably inspires a plethora of romantic associations from elevated affairs of state at the French court to the most sordid practices of ordinary prostitution.

The specimen we encountered was made of white porcelain and sat opposite the usual matching throne in a small room with a marble floor. As if designed by Picasso, the bowl had two mid-length bulges ergonomically and sculpturally shaped for a feminine bottom, a single spigot like a nose and two faucets like eyes polished to a high sheen. The unique installation included a small stainless steel towel rack to my right with two folded face cloths and a small steel shelf on the left with two cakes of up-scale soap, one still wrapped in paper, the other prepared for use. The entire ensemble resembled a smiling face and was most inviting even to a person such as myself equipped with male parts.

I know for a fact that my companion never used it after sex or after anything else. I do not know if its shining presence had any effect on the occurrence of unusually strenuous activities later in the evening. The next morning, I happily felt a certain tension in my abs and real discomfort sitting up. I surreptitiously returned to the head and found some telltale moisture in the bowl as well as a single square of paper and confirmed my suspicions with a gentle question, asked and answered over cappuccino and buttered bread.

SAKE

Ice cold best, aristocratic. Only peasants drink it hot.
I drain it from balsawood boxes
in a ballroom in Kyoto.
All around me businessmen who cut into brains—
doctors of enterprise, who shake your hand
while looking over your shoulder
at the next hello.
Sake was light anesthesia, insurance
against eel sushi and uncooked crustaceans
caught in your teeth. I swallow as much as I can
until my eyes cross, get bleary.

I took my children to a tempura restaurant
in Tokyo where every course was served fried
even the ice cream dessert,
cold at its center and hot on the outside.
I asked how they liked the restaurant
and they just smiled.
O father you are such a simpleton.
I poured another flask of sake icy-hot like a bandage.
I never saw the cauldron boil between the chef's legs
where he dipped our surprise.

Getting Older

The wife knits scarves,
baby blankets, hats for a newborn,
hand warmers, shawls, cowls.
I knit words.
I want an embroidery to *preserve*
a presence that speaks
about an absence.
We sit comfortably in the silence
but for her needles
clicking in the room,
all sound will pass when exactly
we cannot guess—
time undetermined—
not like the old days
of Madame Defarge,
that bitter knitter,
when an end was assigned in ashes
and silence descended with a broom.

SURREALISM COMES WITH AGE

The world and I are parting
like paper pulled from an etching plate.
Each day comes
in a slightly altered state

as if a smear taken from a glass
or a graphite rubbing made from ancient brass.
Breton loved frottage and smoke on a ceiling,
the brown stain of fumage in place of feeling.

Today's copy of yesterday whispers of
but cannot touch love's embodied vision
now turned an apparition
I don't fancy very much.

So raise a glass to how much harder I've become,
a half-living moon turning its back against its sun.

OLD FISH

This morning I woke up and saw an old man's hair
in my ears and nose.

I look in the mirror with eighteen-year old eyes
and see my hair turn gray while I watch.

I rub my fingers against them and know
they are real.

My father's ninety-eight; his hairs hook my lips
kiss by kiss.

Antebellum, antediluvian, prehistoric trilobites all
we generations of phosphorescent fish

in the deepest depths of the ocean,
cowlick sticklers hanging over our eyes,

hope to snare some comely victim's attention,
anything will do but cold respect.

POEM TO A CANE PLACED UPSIDE DOWN

The cleaning ladies leaving the house
have left me a gift, a cane placed upside down
in a corner of the room, its rubber tip aimed at the ceiling,
its L-shaped handle hugging the floor,
a thing strangely smug like Magritte's umbrella.
I ask if it can go for a walk without me, or press
its own spring-loaded buttons in order to grow
taller or shorter, or use someone else's eyes or brain
to navigate? The cane denies everything, yet knows
how often I'm guilty of leaving it behind accidentally
in airports, TSA chasing after me with a cry—
is this your cane Sir, left in the X-ray machine,
not admitting how easily they know it's me
swaying like a drunken sailor aslope on a tilted deck.
I detest our co-dependency, never having been properly
introduced let alone wed. And yet I grow impatient
for my attenuated friend, remembering our last visit
to a museum, how casually we strolled arm in arm
from a wall with a Bonnard to the next Monet.

II

In the dark times
Will there also be singing?
Yes, there will also be singing.
About the dark times.

—Bertolt Brecht, "Motto"
from The Svenborg Poems, 1938

A Poem By Dr. Rieux
(Or Dr. Seuss Meets The Apocalypse)

In quarantine it seemed the obvious thing to do
All of us read The Plague by Albert Camus

But for a critical cow outside the gates going moo
And silent birds flying above our city's zoo

Not many felt disappointed or filled with rue
Spending our days with The Plague by Albert Camus

When the bill for arrogance and greed came due
We paid more in pride than vouchers it's true

What a poor exchange we had made for social glue
Blindness and spite from The Plague by Albert Camus

No more trips to the gym or standing in queues
No unmasked meetings beyond casual ones and twos

No enlightenment came on slow walks to the loo—
All of it foreseen in The Plague by Albert Camus.

[7-21-20]

SOCIAL DISTANCE IN THE CITY

This morning's sun anoints the rooftops
Of the city, washes old brownstones with gold.
We battle an enemy smaller than a hair,
Misplacing our neighbors from lack of caring
And courage. They tell us this is good practice:

Shying from kisses and handshakes, twisting away
From lovers and friends. A few weeks ago
I retired, apparently free from responsibility.
Now I stand masked and six feet distant,
Coughing into my elbow. I wipe gin and T
On our banisters, wash my hands red and raw.

The safety of my walls stokes anxiety in my heart
And irony too: to pull together we must stay apart.

[3-15-20]

A Prayer In The Plague Year

Dear invisible mother can you hear the mourner's Kaddish
I'm saying for you on the anniversary of your death
standing shoeless in my bedroom facing east,
my prayer led by a rabbi and cantor I see streamed
in the invisible ether from a holy temple emptied by fear
of an invisible foe? Dear invisible mother do you hear
the invisible minyan of ten, times ten, perhaps hundreds
standing alone but together in other rooms and houses
praying to an invisible God for rescue and consolation?
Is there enough breath in our song to reach you or Him?
I remember how He saved you in Europe only to take you
too soon in America, and never lived to see a grandchild.
Dear invisible mother make me remember your power
of love and imagination, and see me see me standing here.

[3-21-20]

WALKING THE EDGE OF DEATH

—said by a Wuhan nurse who survived

What we don't know and what we don't need:
Is it better to shut down the economy or proceed;
Is it better to catch a little dose from a crowd
Or suffer alone with your head unbowed;
Does an old drug work or is it just a rumor;
Does the viral dose count or the time of exposure;
Does wearing a mask make things better or worse;
Is it better to give hope or predict a curse;
Is immunity a deadly fib or just a kind of evasion;
Is disunity more dangerous than spiraling contagion;
Is the absence of adulthood a good or evil seed;
Are children really safe from the horrors of disease;
Does ignorance politically succeed?
So much we don't know and so much we won't need.

[4-3-20]

Intensive Care

No figures here but pulse, breath and pressure;
no metonymy of fate but a real hand
cold upon a real sheet.
What could any actor speak more piercing
than this: the dull passage of the day, steady
in its silent leaking through a valve,
passing without acknowledgement,
without an eye-blink or a wave,
just the constant beeping, the mechanics
of death in a noisy room
seven stages above the street
with its rooms full of obdurate facts,
where life once made its living.

[10-26-12/4-10-20]

Every Picture But One

A young wife opens a window in Vermeer,
to let in a pale lemon light at the start of day,
leading the eye through shadows we hear
the gurgle of milk jug, the crinkle of map,
the embroidery twist in its frame as a conductor
might tell his orchestra:
awake softly to the world, my children,
sound flute and horn and drum but sound softly, softly.
The letter she will read has yet to come,
we will never see her milk jug drop and break,
nor her needle tear through the lace.
There's not a smile in any frame:
the maid, the wife and the young man bent
over a keyboard rapt by the day's beginning.

[4-11-20]

No Translations For Love

—Every text remains in mourning until it is translated, Derrida

No texts of mine weep in the Czech of my home country,
a rough language I shamefully never learned
because Mom and Dad spoke it in secret
so as not to interfere with their child's English.
And none of my texts ever yearned for the accent
of those who drove us away, a tongue my father swore
to never voice again, a promise he kept.
Some texts mourn imperfect French, on which I spent
painful years in Brooklyn's public schools,
a skill further confused by my coarse college Spanish,
the lingua franca of conversations with the sick.
Never mind the real pity, hopeless years of Sunday school
and sad pages wishing for Amichai's Hebrew,
especially those poems about you and love and the city.

[4-12-20]

YESTERDAY'S NEWS

Some days during the pandemic
I was so lazy and bored
I read the papers minutes before they became
yesterday's news.
When you're seventy
this is what a fancy prison feels like,
Fed-Med in Baltimore,
no relatives, no friends, no exercise;
even the cat looks bored.
And during Passover week
the same matzoh brei
and coffee milk cereal every day.
The wife and I binge-watched
every British mystery
and the daily medical updates
from Washington and New York.
We were fattening the curves,
hers and mine and the viral attacks
outside where couples still run
six feet abreast.
We wondered how long it would last,
how many weeks would it take to break us,
to push us out into fresh air, shaking hands
with our neighbors and death.

[4-15-20]

THE CLEFT CHIN
—for Jack

I see it every morning shaving
the rugged Bohemian mark in the boys of the family,
my Father's vertical sign passed on
to me and my son and his two little ones
who play in the shade of redwoods
and eucalyptus trees out west.
Too young to guess its possible future meaning,
the power of linked genes for intelligence and melancholy,
the littlest pressed his finger
into the small valley of my chin
whenever we took the plane before.
How I miss that haptic kiss, the apposition of his skin
against mine and the laughter in his eyes.
"What's this," he points and asks
in all innocence of DNA and the power of descent,
in its visible union of past and future. Depressed
I have no response but a silent touch of benediction.

[6-9-2020]

First We Name You

As Adam named each type of person or animal
So we label you before the milk comes
Your first knowledge of the other at her breast
And a rapid succession of toys and books,
Cars and college fill out the rest
Until fully occupied your mind extends
From self to alphabet, from shoelace to stars.
The sole author of your biography
You must write it on other people's faces
In the time and space you have
So that you can truly name yourself
Before all is forgotten at the end:
The milk, the person, and the alphabet,
The generations that came before and after
The oceans and stars and all of creation.

[8-22-20]

The Hours

6 AM:

The cat starts howling at four.
A brisk tail of cooling wraps the house in darkness.
Someone has misplaced the sun. It's Fall.
The day starts later and ends sooner.
The world leans over like a drunken top.
It would be nice to see the planet wake up sooner
And go to bed a bit warmer
Not to be rolled in the cerements of grief, frozen
My alertness stolen moment by moment
As the planet tilts away from the sun's embrace.
And a new year comes for one or the other.

7 AM:

Silent sex at seven is heaven
Even if I must spread my creaky legs too wide
To take you, my groins strained and torn ligaments
Cry. We begin with your furtive search
For a small tube of jellied lubrication
And me pretending not to notice
Though it makes everything feel as good as the old days
Of our youth. Growing older together
Is responsible timing, new wrinkles yoked
To weakening vision. Everything evens out as it fails,
What you don't want me to see I can't see
What you don't want me to do I can't do.

8 AM:

The city traffic unrolls on its asphalt carpet
Symphonic noises, steel plate percussion,
Fluted suspensions and angry trombones.
I can almost hear the concrete crumble
Beneath their wheels, the roaring squadrons
Of autos racing to jobs they mostly hate,
Hoping to get there on time
For a quick coffee and chocolate donut.
America inflates every minute, rush hour stretches
Another hour or two, contracting what's left of life.

9 AM:

Soon this hour will be the hour of lost identity,
The office closed and my bloody uniform returned.
It will be just me, thinning hair and potbelly me
No longer the semi-hero of patients
Nor any attorney's contrary devil, I've escaped
From mountains of unfilled regulatory forms,
Have cut the line to untranslatable phone calls
And uncoil with an anytime breakfast of French toast
And pancakes, hooked on cinnamon and maple syrup,
Depressed by the morning papers of New York
And Baltimore, writing a warrant to find the real me.

10 AM:

In the Gymnasia of either mind or body—
Weight room or desk—I gain as much muscle
And burn off fat working my core or writing it down.
A surgeon has a diurnal rhythm I tell friends,
Better to have your surgery done when everyone's in

A really good mood, especially the man with the knife.
I should know, no longer at work in that valley of anxiety
I pump steel rods and roll wheels on rubber mats
With my trainer DJ, pull TRX cables towards my chest
Made from parachute cords not anchors,
The brain burns more sugar than chopping wood with an axe.

11 AM:

Redbooth data tells us this is the most productive hour
When ten percent of the day's tasks are done
So I must write now, in the hour of least anticipation,
Waiting for lunch at my desk, burning holes in screen glass
Or staring at my empty sheets of paper.
Most days eleven AM is a dry fuck, nothing useful comes
Either hoped for or even unwanted. Then I think
How hours and ours are deadly homophones,
Only the second can run out of the first, not the reverse;
All that belongs to us, whether people or things, must vanish.
At the end of time, all who write become unwritten.

12 Noon:

Every hour speaks of memory. I'm on Greene Street again
Near the churchyard with Poe's grave if not his body in it.
I used to brown bag lunch with peanut butter & jelly
On rye at my big desk or lounge outside the hospital
Inhaling a frank and bun in the bright light bouncing off
Pebbled food carts with aluminum sides before going back in.
Now I'm chained to a more domestic desk waiting for inspiration.
The sun seems high for winter—over the course of an hour
The seasons can change many times.
There's no cinder of an idea in my brain,
No memory that convinces. The self is the deepest mystery
Even as life shortens and my envious eye grows dim.

1 PM:

The hour when the second case started on most busy days—
Operating on someone's spine or through the nose—
The morning case always in the brain already done and closed.
My god I loved that thinking organ like a junkie smoking crack.
Instead I'm getting ready to put the mind's gentler tools away,
Paper and pencil, the computer and its printer spitting out pages
Of half-finished poems and a memoir I've been wrestling for ten years.
I remain neither one thing nor another, my father or my mother,
Artist or scientist or none of the above. It's still me two hours past
My first aliquot of hours, drunk on my beery theme as the day goes on.

2 PM:

The worst time for the brain is early afternoon, a little coffee
Or a power nap may help one snap out of it. On a two-brain day
My students open the head without me, first scalp, then bone
Primping up the field for their professor. I wonder if
The scalp edges bleed too much, is the exposure large enough
To attack a torn vessel or bad tumor? Where are my students anyway?
They are here at the edges of this paper doing the best they can
Without CT or MRI. My sharpened pencil cuts at verbs and nouns,
I can see them cauterizing arteries and veins.
Beneath the microscope I can even smell the burning flesh
Of infinitesimal black threads crossing miniature caverns.

3 PM:

By three o'clock my neurosurgical residents got ready to close
The second head and I this poem. Not likely with hours left to write.
On the first day of my own training, the operation took sixteen hours!
The charge nurse warned me to place a Foley catheter in my bladder
Before I scrub with the slowest surgeon on the staff at Neuro.

Entranced by his sluggish but gentle movements I watch him closely
Remove a tumor almost cell by cell as my bladder filled
With anticipation. The caution of an armadillo
Would remain my watchword throughout the decades:
Never hurry, never make a mistake you can't erase,
Never touch the healthy brain, there's no putting it back together,
His method almost the same as writing one letter at a time.

4 PM:

The hour of the imposter, the afternoon slump gets serious now
For either the one who moves his pens around his desk
Daydreaming about leaving early
Or the medical gunner scrunched down in his foxhole
Anticipating another late evening at the office.
In this hour of transition which track will take hold of me
The train running towards a new disaster
Or back to wife and child? My brain grew wild with romance—
The poem or painting or girl I loved more than daily life,
The cocktail that calmed me and turned off the stress.

5 PM:

As the saying goes, it's always five somewhere in the world—
This most mutable of hours, the eternal hour of the dry martini.
As Churchill prescribed, place glass and gin in the freezer
Hours before you pour, penultimately swipe the lip with lemon pith.
Then carefully step across the room as far as possible
From the dry vermouth because it's never dry enough.
Most of all you must not be on call, must not be caught drinking
With the office staff, must not be in the O.R. at all that day or next.
But writing with a glass on the desk at any hour thereafter is best.

6 PM:

In the old days I was often home by six if not making rounds
On the wards or meeting with my staff.
Not any more—I'm home all day stuck on a preposition
Or a proper word for passing gas.
A thin leaf of paper separates the surgeon and the poet—
It's called a mask. Now I hide behind the metaphor,
The thing I tie up with string,
It's the hope of being understood in the present
That which Emily bound in feathers with a swear
And dropped from an Amherst tower.

7 PM:

In the winter's dusk seven is the darkest hour—
Impossible to banish without headlights pointing
Where I'm going—someone must know
Or suspect the answer of who I am.
One by one the lights come on,
The moon in the east and a single planet costumed as a star.
I'm coming home for dinner before my phone rings again
And breaks the spell of repeating my words over and over
In the car until lines and rhythm sit on my tongue.

8 PM:

We had a beeper back then and not a cellphone.
It called me like a dog to his bone, made me jump if it rang too often.
Sometimes if lucky I turned back for a fractured spine or broken head
And finished by midnight.
While my residents were closing the skin, I wrote poems on a patient's cot
Outside the O.R. door until something flamed up and caught.
Or if I couldn't scrub out, sang the words to myself

Until I stripped off my gown and found pencil and paper.
Not everything survived until then—
I could always remember the art I saw but not the words I sought.

9 PM:

With morning rounds and surgery in the offing
I couldn't stay up too late. Back then I went to bed at nine,
Watching the news and reading one detective story
After another, my wife always out cold by ten.
Now I'd be a night owl if I were able
Who can't enjoy the lateness of the hour
Because of age. Instead I keep a journal by my bed
But wake more often to pee than scrawl a poem.
Still the lines I steal from sleep are among my best
And the ones that come during drowsing even better.
Poincaré used beauty as a test to solve equations while he slept
Or walked with Newton on a beach and found a perfect shell.

10 PM:

At the wolf's hour I grow accustomed to doubt;
There are no plans to hang me though many have their reasons,
Among them former students, publishers and lawyers.
They hate my surgical certainty, the way I whisper
At the top of my lungs or worry how loud I sing,
How dramatically I read my poems.
Not wishing my life to look like hoi polloi
I stay up too late as the hours turn
And feel morbid and unsettled instead.

11 PM:

I tremble as if the blade's hour has come. But it was dawn
Not midnight when beheading before an audience was done
In Revolutionary France and Nazi Germany. Two families served
As executioners, the Sansons from 1792 to 1847 and the Deiblers,
Louis and Anatole, chief headsmen from 1879 to 1939.
More than 16,500 people were killed by guillotine before 1945.
The Angel of Death is famous, so why not his henchmen? Myself
I've never seen the head of a chicken cut off by a farmer's wife.
The National Razor of France was scrubbed in 1977. What did the head
In a basket see, if brain activity in decapitated rats lasts seconds more—
This doesn't mean sense just a stupid reflex in a dumb beast.
Aren't we like rats huddling in our cages, don't victims always think
They're safe? This was the science the Germans knew before killing us.

12 Midnight:

Sleepless in the blackest hour of the night,
I sometimes take out a special book or think
With regret about the one I'll never see in life,
It's The Duke of Berry's *Very Rich Hours*,
Two hundred calfskin pages, a foot tall each,
Locked away in Chantilly's vault.
Most of the leaves are painted with ruby red,
Aqua-blue or gold on ermine white,
Complete with calendars and prayers
For the canonical hours,
Also Bible stories and David's psalms,
As perfect and as incomplete as any
Sacrifice made by Abraham.
The project ended when the Limbourg Brothers
And their sponsor died with Plague, their deep
Devotion unrewarded but for posthumous fame.

1 AM:

The last hour in the scholar's study, I am reading:
The declension of French verbs, the collective nouns of animals,
Atoms and molecules, and the secrets of the benzene ring.
Also the gene I first met in a bar like a bad date,
Facts like worms encysting in my brain. And even worse—
Philosophy goes home with the exhausted undergrad.
Will I be found at two, my still warm body lying on the floor?
That too much knowledge can kill is a mystery without a plot.
In *The Hours*, Cunningham links Virginia Woolf,
Mrs. Dalloway and HIV, choosing to defeat the tyranny of Time
With close observation over suicide. As for us,
The poet and his reader are always alone adjusting our clocks.

2 AM:

By two or three I make the first of several trips to the head
And, holding myself in one hand, dribble slow, so slowly
There's plenty of time to think of myself as a younger man
In the nightlight's shadow. But this is no time for regret.
I can't see the faces of the past even with my eyes closed
And must make it back quickly before the rest
Of me wakes up or worse, I hit a shin on the bed frame
And wake my wife.
Two was the worst of hours for an emergency call from Shock Trauma,
The residents and I discussing how to stabilize the patient
Until morning, the darkness filling my veins with so much drama
I could never return to sleep again.

3 AM:

It might seem an ordinary thing
Not to be able to see the bathroom light at three in the morning,
My eyelids closed as if sleep were death,
My eyelids thicker than thin.
Where to begin a little understanding, catecholamines roiling
The antipodes of feeling, appalling both stomach and brain.
The next day I'm taken for an eye examination,
No retinal tears or buckling seen just arteries and veins.
In the bright slit of a retinoscope my doctor looks at the center
Of my world and I feel the first or last of life exploding.

4 AM:

The next darkest hour, a final absolute obliteration of light
Before the world scrambles back with its diurnal high
Of cortisol and your grumbling stomach wakens you
With worry about the first case you've posted
On the O.R. schedule and all the ways it might go wrong.
Or else some other matter frightens you more
Than ordinary nightmare, the sale of a beloved possession,
A car or boat or home, a first meeting that evening
With a potential daughter- or son-in-law,
A dinner with your spouse and the lawyer she's screwing.
There's no poison more powerful than imagination.

5 AM:

The hour of hanging in the subcontinent; I wake up on my own
Like a prisoner marching out to meet his fate.
At cock's crow the alarm goes off, the starter's gun for another race,
The blurred beginnings of new futures.
I reach my hand out to shut it down but it's too late,

The hours have begun their ordinary run from dawn to darkness,
The numbers steadily climbing up the Day. Most waiting
Breathless at our job, whatever it might be, a line of sutures
Or a line of poetry, for the judgement of others as to how we rate.
Why do we care? Is not the work hard enough without the pain?
But we are social animals who must die, our glory and fate.

III

Art is a line around your thoughts—Gustav Klimt

WHITE SPACE

From time to time, you find the center
at the margins, all meaning between the lines
where sunlight streams through the slats
of a blind.

In the beginning, it took only a few words
to make sunlight, meaning—
no audience, no preaching,
a rule He understood.

We ourselves might take back creation
a word at a time,
editing out fathers and mothers
even the first murder of a brother.

Then came the soul-breaching of city walls,
of illness, of belated discovery
when a true lover has departed, is gone.

In the white space of the city,
your hands land like plums on my back,
and the room goes blank.

A Memory Of Málaga

—at the Picasso Museum

To your left an old painter's hand has conjured up
the picture of him on his burro;
it looks enough like the child
Pablo Ruiz Picasso
his yesterday collapses into tomorrow.

Nearby hang the flounced sleeves of his lover
Dora Maar mixed with sand—
an ocean of desire on its falling edge
in a great wave of green color—
fucked in life she fucks in paint.

On your right his first wife Olga depicted
as earth mother, the dark side of her face
birthing a suspicious demon
raised in Málaga by a professor father
who gave up his palette and paint box
to the man-child asleep in her lap.

This autobiography crushes my eyes,
stirs a disturbing wish, a criminal need to touch
a vase of flowers and a plate of cakes
Pablo made from a teapot and metal clamp:
its evil petals studded with nails, decorated
with ceramic pastry, he chewed on and spit up

in the heat of a single day, his mighty furnace
baking his veins into iron and clay.

CLEMENT GREENBERG,
LIVING IN MY HEAD RENT FREE

Before and after the single evening spent together
touring a solo show in the Fuller Building
and one or two years before his death,
he lives in my head
like a field mouse off the street in winter.
That evening, at the young artist's opening,
we first sat in the back office, me opposite his desk
staring at his cane and sneaking a look at his face,
mouth twisted by years of New York Yiddish.
We waited for the artist,
dressed like a dominatrix in black jodhpurs
and boots, to clear away her friends
so she might do a walk-around with Clem and me.

We'd already inspected her work
in the otherwise empty front room, remarking on the way
she painted herself in a bell-shaped gown
like the *infanta* Margaret Theresa in Velázquez
whether attending a ball or surrounded by animals in a forest,
a sort of weak-tea Surrealism with glowing eyes from the Forties,
how she left the grey *pentimenti* of her under-drawing visible
like the more mysterious paintings of David Salle or Degas.

Clem told me he'd gladly promote a realist if only he could find one
as good as Velázquez or Vermeer but because he hated *kitsch*
was "stuck" with Pollock, Mondrian and Newman.
We waited thirty minutes or more
for her to free herself from adulation and admirers
and Clem was getting tired on his throne. At his request
I pushed my way to her and said
you don't understand, Mr. Greenberg—Clement Greenberg—
wants to walk around and discuss your work with you!

She couldn't be bothered and I knew why,
he'd already spent thirty years as the most hated man in the art world,
he believed in Kant and Hegel and Marx, and I believed in him
and his theory. Fearfully I returned to my seat in front of the desk
and gave him the news. He wasn't surprised.
After he left, I made my escape and closing the door heard the walls
screaming *you don't understand Michael, it's all kitsch today.*

Pictures On A Trembling Wall

—for Jack Whitten, 1939-2018

On the big dining room wall a desperate man
and woman once stabbed their way
through a wild river smoking with rain;
they left a faded patch of gray until
a triptych of Serrano photographs moved in,
its three parts sporting a single arc of jism
shot in space and timed to a camera
like the galloping gait of a nineteenth century horse.
The struggling swimmers briefly returned,
(after all, we ate in this room) before a final banishment,
and Whitten's black acrylic slab took up all the space
and air, never to let go, hugging the wall
with a sense of desperation, dissected by a grate
of vertical ravines dug with an African hair comb.
This painting held the memories of its making:
an image of a metal door hinge or shackle Jack had placed
beneath the canvas troweling plastic resin
and floating flickers of blue and yellow paint
soaked from torn Japanese woodcuts.
In between the bars some gray and white
but not enough to erase its black prisonous aroma
nor the demand the painting makes for looking harder.
I gave it a proper stare, feeling all it had replaced:
his city's streets and towers, and the pulse of a river rising,
even the fear of that couple drowning
as if they might escape nature's wildness to enter his cage.

Mannequins

—for Gabriele Leidloff, Berlin

The X-ray of the most beautiful girl in the world
reveals a rod in her leg, a pin in her shoulder,
her ice-blue face smooth as water
cascading down the forehead of a glacier.

The X-ray of the most beautiful girl in the world
is the lit-up face of a death mask,
its brow as broad as Goethe,
with the smile of a sybil who never was,
trussed like a prisoner bursting free.

The X-ray of the most beautiful girl in the world
displays her legs in a balletic plie,
her arms akimbo
like a sailor at rest.
Or a corpse thrown into a ditch
machine-gunned in a Russian forest.

The X-ray of the most beautiful girl in the world
is a cipher of plaster dissolved in radium,
of movement immobilized,
of passion unrealized,
of a dream that never was and always is.
The most beautiful girl in the world is an X-ray.

(1997)

A Painting Called "Winter"
—after Frank Bowling, 1977

At its left edge a comet of neon yellow and ochre drips down
a green ground abutting a broad violet pillar, itself overlaid
with an oscillating scrawl of pink botanicals, like an EEG
turned on its side in a seizure of electrical interference.
How did the title come to mind after pouring Spring colors
on a canvas tilted side to side and up to down?
Perhaps it was done in opposition to the reality he saw outside
his studio windows, the glow of light on a frozen river,
the sky's reflection in neighboring towers or else a memory
of early days without support for gas or coal. There's no restraint
in what he would do at any time to clear the cold from his mind,
like Turner's black mood turning watery ripples into fire.

CORRESPONDENCE: DEEP YELLOW-GREEN
—after a tondo by Leon Polk Smith, 1967

There are only two possibilities:
Either the shadow of an orange sun has fallen
On the green earth or
An orange moon is partially occluded
By a green sun;
Either the orange scimitar is turning
Around a green ball
Or the ball is spinning out of an orange disc.
Either everything is moving or everything is still.
There are only two possibilities.

His Name Meant Light

—for Tom Lux (1946-2017)

I never knew how he got his name, but he wore it well:
Lux as in *shining* on or *revelatory*,
not just insubstantial photons, also fleet footed
as in how he ran the bases or scooped up balls
in the outfield, not evanescent.
In his poems obsolescent or humble
things were treated as people:
for example the virgule or a mouth full of rotten teeth—
but could never turn people into objects.

Tom radiated so much respect he cursed at you
out of kindness in order to save your gift.
An elegy titled *Stinkface* might have served him better
than this one, he'd laugh a little
and give fate a look you could smell whenever
you did something stupid—
like stepping on my cat,
or being startled by the news of his unexpected death,
two creatures howling
and bereft, shocked how sickness had crept
into those mighty lungs of declamation
and stilled those ropey-veined arms.

I can still see Tom booming every pitch
against a stone wall in center field;
he's probably still hitting balls out to right
where Frost patrols or left where Emerson
manicures the grasses.
He loved their mottoes of excellence,
and was ecumenical about most subjects
except the Shoah—he felt all poems on the subject
weak or strong, deserved a roomful of respect.

I thought he made it up, that perfect name
and metaphor against ignorance and doubt.
We were born the first year after the world's worst war
and never forgot its darkness. He fought it better than I did
with a joyous grin and an ancient grandfather with the genes
of a Bohemian pig farmer. He wore it well,
that bright lamp of illumination, *Lux Aeterna*.

Summer Conference With D.D.

—for Deborah Digges (1950-2009)

At the end of the week I'd written ten—
a poem in two voices, a poem about objects seen far away
and up close in magnification.
I've never been able to do that again.
You said *read them to me*, making a few quick edits
and lightning fast struck a comma here, a word there.

Then you said *read them again*,
closing the bud vase of your face, shuttering its stare.
Leaning back to listen
your lips moved in and out with each iamb,
above the upper a single drop of quivering moisture
and a ten-mile pile of red hair, already graying.

Thirty minutes in, you came out of your spell
and said we were done. I was dismissed as if only
a disciple blessed by your touch,
by the hand that ordinarily swept away
invisible sparrows you heard for years speaking in tongues,
shadowed in the one treeless plaza on campus.

Who was I to argue? In your weakness was your strength
and having your ear that day as good as sex
(though somehow it felt like a death in childhood.)
Done, we were done, you sooner than most—
like that bee that stung in Plath. I gave you my thanks
and moved on, my palms growing as red as strawberry jam.

JOHN UPDIKE'S TRASH

Discovered: honorary diplomas from Dartmouth, Bates,
Emerson and Salem State, bound for the dump;
boxfuls of cancelled checks,
a buck thirty-four from the Screen Actors Guild
in exchange for a Simpson's voiceover,
Christmas cards from presidents Bush and Clinton,
John Lithgow and Elliot Richardson—
a partial list of ephemera filched from Updike's waste stream
in which a stranger dips with helpless glee.
Paul Moran, onetime resident of Salem, Mass
scoops up family snaps, explicit love letters, underpants,
an address book, floppy disks from a Wang computer,
notes for an unpublished novel about St. Paul,
the saint and not the city I would guess.

Three years spent rooting through Updike's garbage cans
gives a more private view of him, skewing away
from the rectitude of his public portrait, saying gone
to the politesse, the nasal tone, his Puritan's view of sex.
Today, the collector and his wife operate Maui Wowee,
a tropical ice-stand in Austin.
Imagine the writer walking up to buy a rainbow cone,
looking at Moran for a possible role in his next novel.
Moran declines this offer and modestly names
his on-line site The *Other* John Updike Archive, as if
any biographer would pass by such a treasure
and its repository of regret,
the humble mirror of what we excise
pointing back at how *we* felt about what we kept.

Twelve Reflections On Francis Picabia (1879-1953)

I-*The devil follows me day and night because he is afraid to be alone.*

> Even under a sunless sky I am chased by my shadow;
> at each street corner
> one of us smiles, the other laughs or cries.

II-*Pain has its reasons, pleasure is totally indifferent.*

> Pain is automatic and protective; a simple toothache signals
> deep into the brain.
> Pleasure is a dangerous accident, nerve endings twitch
> At a frequency I can't remember.

III-*If you want to have clean ideas, change them as often as you change your shirts.*

> I don't have enough shirts and must scrub my brain free from old ideas.
> A clean brain fractures like parchment, revealing a mirage in the desert,
> the brain as a metaphor making machine.

IV-*My ass contemplates those who talk behind my back.*

> We all have our critics. The composer Max Reger responded like this:
> "I sit in the smallest room in my house,
> your review is before me, soon it will be behind me."

V-*We are ignorant of our acts until we accomplish them.*

> This is how Dada worked—Picabia did all the talking,
> Marcel got all the fame; two leopards in the same cage
> one always changing his spots while the other wouldn't.

VI-*Between my head and my hand, there is always the face of death.*

The execution of a thought takes time
often a minute, sometimes a year, rarely an entire life
until there are no thoughts and no time.

VII-*The only way to win is to fight on the side of your adversaries.*

I'm like the spies Joshua sent to Jericho.
My loved ones think I'm invisible or deaf and can't hear them plotting.
I am not like smoke or air or words, I have a shape, even a smell.

VIII-*The essence of a man is found in his faults.*

Filled with faults like a volcano or tectonic plates
I'm greedy, envious, dreaming of alternative lovers I will eat
like a lion on a dry plain.

IX-*Only useless things are indispensable.*

I collect battle ribbons and old toys, Matryoshka that no longer surprise.
I remember wooden wheels and gears stuck together by plastic tubes
a child once built into machines, the same masterpiece over and over.

X-*Our heads are round so our thoughts can change direction.*

A square head points two ways at once, back to the future
or forward to the past.
Like a snail's slimy trail we ignore the present.
I am the evidence. Thank you for your patience.

XI-*Good taste is as tiring as good company.*

This is a true story, not a joke: three artists take a ride
into the French countryside.
It's July of 1912 and Picabia drives (after all, it's his car);
Debussy and Apollinaire sit in the back egging him on
about the fiction of pure painting, pictures without subjects.
Picabia drinks a lot and rushes back to his studio
where he changes abstraction from a verb to a noun.
He later says *My painting is a contest between life and sleep.*

XII-Knowledge is an old error remembering its youth.

In his long life Picabia makes many errors
and gains much knowledge but little wisdom.
He wrote *paralysis is the first stage of wisdom*
but lived like a comet in constant motion.
He was not like us but we are like him.

[Section titles and two lines in italics are bon mots by Francis Picabia]

SELF PORTRAIT AS SERF

—after Matisse, *The Serf, 1900-1908*

Serf—not a name I would have chosen for this mighty bronze:
neither helot nor semi-slave nor villein bound to the earth
but a man striding forth at the dawn of a new age

besieged by science and Cézanne.
In an early snap the bearded Serf stands naked to his labor
like his master does, artist and statue looking much the same,

two unchained Stankovites laboring. Matisse took this alter ego
from Rodin's *Walking Man*, first hiring the master's
favorite model, Bevilaqua, for a portrait in paint.

From paint to clay he transposed the flat patches of color
of one into the muscled blocks of the other,
edges angled and cut by a palette knife sharp as light,

the new man of a new century bricked up like an artillery tower
or battering ram with legs attached.
In an eight-year campaign, the plaster remained uncast

until one day, in a fit of malice, Matisse snapped off its arms
and watched his deformed monster grow in strength
like ancient Venus erupting in beauty after her amputation.

THE KNIFE THROWER

—after Jazz by Matisse, 1947

They must have thought he'd gone insane,
the old man too sick to paint, lying in his bed,
a turban perched upon his head

and colored papers piled around him.
Matisse wrote a friend *I'll need a white cane,*
gone blind from cutting into color this way,

bright spirals and chits falling off his scissors.
He made a book of jazzed-up clowns and kings
floating lagoons and tropical plants,

its acrobats and rearing horses, too big to hold
in his hands, land smiling across his lap.
But deep beneath the circus paint a cry, a frown:

a man who swallows a sword, his pain
starred in his eye, a magician winding up to throw
a knife at his lavender assistant splayed

against the wall. He's coiled like a snake,
hot pink on blue and beige, caught in the moment
before letting go. And all around, leaves and ferns

are raining down—one boxed in white
where her heart should be, its shape an obvious target
for his knife's velocity, her arms thrown up and still.

Think of Manet and the firing squad
in the *Fifth of May*, Goya in the *Disasters of War*,
think of the years Matisse survived: his wife living apart

and the smoke still cooling on all the battles of his life.

EPIPHANY

Oh James Franco, I don't know
at first you seemed such a special fellow—
three PhDs and two MAs
and a movie you cut off your arm in.
I was certain you had an identical twin
busy on a hook in the closet.
Then came your poetry book and worse
a starring turn
in *Of Mice and Men.*
Revelation came on the last day of your play,
when we were swamped
in a crowd so thick
we couldn't move or breathe,
dozens of airborne phones flashing
to catch a flick of you, James Franco,
my epiphany—
your portrait as good as a selfie,
their identification complete.
You could almost hear the screams:
see me, see me, please.

THE GOOD TOURIST

Near the end of my life, I realized I was a good tourist, loved almost every place I visited in person including, most surprisingly, every city in Germany and Japan. Of course I loved all of Italy and France, but unsure about Madrid. I hated Vienna. Like Goya I have an allergy to the Hapsburg Empire and its lantern jawed proto-fascists who built palaces out of stones taller than my shoulder with doornails bigger than my head. I could never spell Lipizzaner stallion correctly and only pretended to like Sacher torte even though I first ate it at the Hotel Sacher and my brain loves chocolate like an essential amino acid. Average people in Hapsburg days were quite small and had trouble getting around the streets if they didn't have a horse and carriage and drivers with whips who also cleaned up the horse shit; no wonder Freud loved Vienna and his patients dreamed dreams of escape. Most sadomasochists, including Freud, liked to get out and visit Prague, a city with its own problems, one that gave Kafka nightmares. You have to know a town as nice as Prague really well to become as afraid of it as Kafka, but even a stranger can feel in summer, against all the laws of thermodynamics, that the buildings of Vienna radiate a deep chill that compensates for the lack of air conditioning in many banks, where the physiognomy of the pouched out, pockmarked stones recapitulates the dour psychology of the citizens, most of whom look like old Nazi pensioners. As far as I can tell, no one looked like Orson Welles. I fell in love with Amsterdam and Ghent. I saw Jerusalem right after an intifada and Rio before the Zika virus. Everywhere in the Caribbean and South America I was welcomed by the native citizens, even by a blue-footed booby in the Galapagos after I twisted my ankle landing on its volcanic shore. I was mostly a good tourist. I'm sorry I never made it to Africa or Australia and never saw a polar ice cap or even Alaska. Then there's Vienna. I often think about Walter Benjamin, how he killed himself at midnight on the wrong side of the Pyrenees. A good tourist, I forgive a lot, but not everything.

IV

A book is not supposed to be a mirror. It's supposed to be a door.
—Fran Lebowitz

Event Horizon

There's no such thing as eternity
When the sun explodes there goes Leonardo
And the Fifth Avenue Library
And all those unsold piles of books
In my basement.
Will anybody be reading the Bible
On Alpha Centauri
Or looking at a Picasso sent by rocket?
Who will grieve for the oceans or the ants
And those little countries no bigger than rocks
We never learned the names of?
No more bucket lists and no more buckets.
Just an empty space filled with humility
And a master builder looking for the switch.

How The Professor Rose

Quick as an otter and half as slick,
Professor H. swanned behind his lectern
in a classroom filled with future surgeons
and psychiatrists.

Dressed like an earl, he pulled himself up
so that we could see his face,
the big head and little body,
his creamed hair smoothed back as if
he'd smartly cracked a clam.

A mostly benevolent Peter Lorre
without the lisp, he made his class
a gory 1930s hour—
Hitchcock in a hemistich.

I thought he'd eat me with those store-bought teeth
from London, the smiling grille
of a 60's Buick in a New England mouth.

Day by day he rose and rose
in the same blue suit, pointy-toed Oxfords
and club tie, poppet body lifting
with the regularity of a metronome

but never a note taller.
He hoped to convert us to a humanist's view
beyond medical science and graded harshly.
He knew true humility would come later
at the hands of patients
in an amputated alphabet that began with B.

THE MUSCLES ON THE MUSCLE MAN

—after Vesalius

Think of them as flaming sarcomeres, of wings,
As anything but meat spilled in an abattoir,
Think of them as freed from gravity, from age
From death, from all the ailments angels fear
And run from, from adrenal dystrophy and polio
From myasthenia, from central core disease
From all and anything that stops us on our way,
These mighty agents of movement unspooled,
Their severed tendons hanging like bandages,
Like scarves in the wind or ribbons won
In a race long ago ended, the motors of the body
Gigantic placed in a landscape by Leonardo,
The head turned away in grief at so many secrets
Revealed, hung by a pulley hung from a beam.

In The Morgue

The diener cuts her from ear to ear
and pulls down the scalp over her eyes.
He takes up the drill to prise off the skull cap
revealing the treasure inside.

I watch him split her hemispheres apart
until a soft bruise appears in the frontal lobe
where late I entered a fateful journey
to what Descartes opined was the soul's own throne

and found disaster, like Rider's *She*
or the snakes uncoiling in Solomon's mines.
Here the walnut-sized answer grew in a natural void
covered by a custard of telephone lines

our brains employ for silent speaking
and holding us together.
I'd missed the tumor's center and she had died
by my mistake—this was the riddle.

Had I overstretched the surface veins
until they clotted, drowning her mind
in a viscous wave of slowing blood
or lost myself in her anatomy?

Her burdens were mine. We wanted to know not hide
what went wrong, expose the cause of catastrophe
but this was not to be.
As it does in life the brain kept safe its mystery.

Heard In A Museum: John Cage Sonatas

Temple bells in Ryoan-ji;
raked sand. The rake.

An ant beats on a log;
thunder in Tibet.

Beneath a waterfall, the water gourd;
a broken necklace.

The clock made of confetti,
gray leaves, dented cans.

Sharaku's actor advances his knife;
the gamelan screams.

Leopards in the jungle walk on
broken glass, pots and pans.

A cymbal wears mittens;
a toothless cylinder in a music box.

Sunset in Papua; sunrise
in Manhattan.

Out pops a ribbon and 30 screws
hidden in the strings. Steve Reich's trains.

A bolt flies out of the piano frame,
the sound spills like soap.

A man with a monkey face
hangs before me; Rembrandt frowns.

Savor slowly. You might not live to hear this
ever again.

BALTIMORE'S EAST SIDE

Behind our backs, even to your face, some called it *Jewtown*—
this where the crowds pushed out onto the sidewalks
by big fancy cars made you sweat like a beaver.
Live chickens in cages, fish in shop windows,
lambs hung at Passover and Easter, and a side show of gawkers
and mamzers, rabbis and shmendriks. In so much noise
intonation was everything: a *nu* to a stranger might mean
asking for his passport, a *nu* with a shrug foreplay to your wife.
There were a thousand ways to say stupid in Yiddish,
(not all of them nice) squeezing a melon or sneezing
and spitting too close to pickle barrels on East Lombard,
the street which gave in to a century of change.

Called Jones Town after the Irish and Germans came,
it flipped its name when the Jews, Italians and blacks arrived,
working like slaves in the East Side canneries, breweries,
sweatshops and trains before high rises, public housing,
and crime swept away the white stoops and brownstones.
The old neighborhood died with King in riots and flames.
Then we moved to the suburbs and our gang lost its taste
for Yankelove's Poultry, Waltzman's bagels, and cream cheese
at Smelkinsin's. All that was left were three delicatessens,
two shuls and the sickened teeth of stand-alone houses. Today
no one goes to Fineblum's for candy or Talkoff's for fruit,
no one dates at the Educational Alliance. It's as quiet as The Pale.

BLOWN UP

Three thousand pounds of explosive packed into a truck
make a big noise.
First conscious then knocked out by flying debris,
hiding in a building a hundred yards downstream,
when the acoustic wave blows him into the air like a rubber ball,
every day since then headaches wake him up at night
or flashbacks do.

This is the thing, he's thirty-three,
says if I make him well he will go right back to Iraq,
back to Fallujah or some dark mountain in Afghanistan
where an IED ten years ago first silenced his brain momentarily.
Now the fourth blow of a suicide bomber has struck
this man as big as a tree, disrupted his life.
He fights back his memories and tears.

We shake hands and I softly disappear into his pink palm,
like a robin returning to its nest.
They call it a theater of operations as if it were a play.
Now his head stores backstage all the scenery
and special effects, that bright star of pain behind
his left temple. The anxious shards of liquefied glass
and shadows make sand in his head. PTSD.
This will pass, I say, without hope that it will.

Blind Spot

Ill named. We all have one—
seeing depends on it—
in the back of the eye
where the gift of sight enters
a sink of nervous tissue
and shape and size and color
drain towards the brain.
I see it daily
this spot
where we divine
the world,
with lens and light
before their eyes.
I force myself
on its pink punctum
of arteries and veins.
No elevated pressure I say
as if to relieve you of anxiety.
But the headaches still come.
Imaginary pain is still pain.

Lies Before Retirement

The last patient lies to me (of course):
about never having had headaches before,
about not being depressed,
about how well he slept
before the accident,
before he fell on a wet floor at work
and tapped the left side of his head
like a finger on a desk.

The lawyers for my last deposition
shave the truth as smooth as a peach
(of course). I'm closing the store—
soon I will take down all my diplomas,
gaudy posters of Seventies' art shows,
and a few certificates of competence.

No one including myself can guess
what I feel, beavering after truth,
a half century of healing ended
mirroring the hardships of others,
stripping away layers of falsehoods
like a detective with a scalpel
digging at fears we hold in common.

INSISTENCE

Here. Eat this now, take these words
into your belly— that's what God said
to Ezekiel while he gave him a scroll
for his mouth;

that's what you say when my hands
are already filled with chores of my own; *eat this now*
as if I had a third hand free to take your cup
of woe and unload you of your duty.

Give me the remote, you say,
Give it to me now, even though the speakers
are painfully loud and I can't cover my ears
fast enough while you figure it out.

After you fall sleep, I watch your lips flutter
with breath, red like Tiepolo's angel;
I want to kill you there and then
you know, but brush my teeth instead.

Reversal

Screenwriters call it a reversal:
the audience expecting one thing
gets another, like when William Devane
rescues Dustin Hoffman's mouth
from Laurence Olivier's drill
in *Marathon Man*—and almost instantly
proves part of the conspiracy.

His deceit's the least part of the horror
we feel like a thrill—a reversal
of our natural wish to seek comfort, a state
as ignorant as a flower turning towards the sun.

Hypnotized, we re-orient towards what we fear,
worship an idol that will eat us—recall only
the prophecy given Alexander:
live forever, die young.

Wounds

There are those who lost everything and almost everyone
who did not lose themselves

And those who lost themselves and lost nothing.

There are those who lost a little and remained whole
and those who lost almost nothing and were destroyed.

There are those who lose something and never find it again
and those who were lost from the start.

There are those who cannot know what they never had
and those who never hear their own still voice.

Loss happens a lot but God doesn't choose what we lose.

The Empty House

I once stayed in a friend's house without even a can of soda
at hand, a not so mysterious shell
because there's no one to purchase the groceries
and no one who lives there who can bear to eat them.

So there's nothing to drink in the house of mourning
and no one who visits really wants a drink—well
you know what's coming.

The house sits in the midst of a tame and terrible desert—
true story—
as luxurious as the antechamber of Hell,
a subdivision on the edge of a historic city,
and its front gate has a welcome bell
rung coming and going
but not by me.

Since this is a true story there's not much else to tell.
The owner lives elsewhere, paralyzed
but moving; he's afraid to sell.

SELECTED POEMS
FROM THE FIRST FOUR BOOKS

Writing a book is a horrible, exhausting struggle,
like a long bout with some painful illness.
One would never undertake such a thing if one
were not driven on by some demon one can
neither resist nor understand.
—George Orwell, *Why I Write*, 1946

From
The Clock Made Of Confetti
(2007)

PERFECT

This is what we meant for it to be—
backing out of the brain,
letting eloquent lips close over
the small spitting heart of a bruised vessel
recently clipped shut
or hiding the bed from which unruly cells
had been wrestled, removing ourselves
and our miniature extensions, closing
the *dura mater* with a crotchet of sutures
as if zippering a body bag
over a person's head, replacing the lid
of sawed bone, sprinkling its dust into holes
pneumatically drilled four hours ago,
after lifting a dog-ear of muscle
and cutting a semicircle of scalp and skin
with blade and hot smoking wire,
from just in front of an auricle
to just above a brow, and now, now
no longer looking in but looking out
at the soul propped up in bed, its crown
of bandages turbaned and taped,
its eyelids bruised and closed
with seepage, its mostly successful struggle
to awake in minutes, in hours,
even the next day, applauded as perfect
by our own exhausted eyes.

SITTING SHMIRA

Outside the morgue on First
and Thirtieth street, a canopy
has been erected next to
three truck-loads of mixed body parts.
Under the tent, teams of young
yeshiva girls
sit shmira, watching over the dead
in four hour shifts.
What should take only a day
has gone on for eight or nine weeks.
Since no one knows
who's in these trucks,
the dead cops, candy vendors,
bond traders and unsuspecting passersby,
all the uncommon inhabitants
of our one earth's island
are assumed converted by fire and ash
into one Jew, one blood, and one flesh.
Since no one can be buried like this,
no one can be properly mourned.
But hour after hour, the sweet melodies
of psalms rise over the conversos
until a light is lit in David's garden,
a moon with a broken edge,
its author as anonymous as any victim.

FISH TALKS, TOWN BUZZES—
New York Times, 3-15-03

For the sake of drama, it would be nice to think
Luis Novelo almost chopped his hand off
when the fish began to speak,
instead he dropped a rubber mallet used to stun
the carp with and fell against the wall
sliding on to slimy packing crates that covered
the floor. No one in Equador spoke Hebrew
but he knew it when he heard it
having worked in Mr. Rosen's shop
for seven years. He thought it was the devil
speaking in the cat's throat, thrown
from another room or from the slop sink,
from anywhere but a fish. He flung it back
into the ice box and still it spoke; Luis yelled
and soon enough Mr. Rosen heard it too—
the voice of God, he thought
or even Mr. Lifshitz, a holy man
who died last year, come back to fret about
his town and its morals.
Zalmen heard the old Hasid say "study Torah
and pray, the end is near". All those years
the man bought carp for Shabbos
and never said a word; now this.
How he hated those silvered lips!
Mr. Rosen tried to kill it with a cleaver
but the soul of Mr. Lifshitz bucked off
the counter and fell into the carp box,
snuggling down with its iced-off
brethren. Zalmen almost cut his thumb off
and had to be taken away in an ambulance.
A psychiatrist asked—

was it a Purim prank or a mass hallucination?
What does it mean when God's word
is made manifest in a twenty pound carp,
then butchered and sold for appetizer?
Abraham Spitz, the town's only lawyer said
"Two men do not dream the same dream."

A BLEAK AND GAUDY CARNIVAL

I saw the last home run in Boston, that last at bat
before he vanished into ponds and rivers, as fine
a fisherman as ever mounted a punt or waded
a stream to cast a fly. No longer slim, he swung back
like a snake coiled on a leather-clad pediment,
his legs so twisted in fury, you could feel the cold
cast of his supernatural eye. Well before John Henry
had him shipped from Hernando to that cryogenic lab
in Scottsdale, his fondest wish was to feed the speckled trout
one last time, to mix his ashes with his old dog
Slugger's, and float above their heads, a hand-tied
damsel dancing on air, a slim wooly worm on the fly.
Instead, the old atheist hangs upside down in a vat
of liquid nitrogen, while decapitated heads float
above him, and star bursts of ice explode in his cells
until hope is only a molecule.
But technology is too weak a brew; no chip of DNA
can bring him back, no splinter make our sons
and daughters any better than we expect—
his own misnamed son had the full genetic load
and all he got from Ted was misplaced pride.
With all due respect, John Henry couldn't hit God's fast ball
to save himself; all of us old enough have tried.

The Clock Made Of Confetti

It takes a long time, all those blossoms
had to bloom and die—first
the star-shaped forsythia swept under
by red and white azalea petals
scattered like confetti,
the morning after a big party
when no one remembers what
they're celebrating.
Then the pink crab apple had to let go
its love notes, lately interred
with a white Bradford pear.
There were more who fell
than I can remember
embraced by age and the slow pull
of gravitation: cicada shells I kicked
out of my way and the brown wren
too small for this winter, brought down
by some marauding cat.
I repeated your name each day
until snow covered the lawn
with its white leopard's breath,
and when it melted and spring came,
I knew you were gone.

LADY HEART

I've opened the O.E.D. and found
lady's apple, lady's cushion,
lady finger, lady's glove,
lady-silver, lady's laces,
lady's longing, lady's mantle,
lady smock, lady's seal,
lady's slipper, lady's thistle,
and lady's tresses but no
mention of a lady's heart anywhere.

Is there a flower named lady heart?
I think I see one over there—
a three-leafed pink held up
by Lancelot in a medieval
tapestry. He offers it
to Guinevere, her gown of green sable
athwart her white steed,
her neck washed white,
naked of sun.

And here's another,
displayed in a book
of imaginary ills,
written by a hypochondriac.
They're pulling a tooth
and the surgeon's arrayed
a sprig of pinks around his room
to give off a bouquet of courage;
it's pictured on a page
surrounded by pincers and saws.

Photography: A First Course

A tableaux of figures in a mirror
bubbles slightly like old glass;
beneath the chromate, pass generations.
It takes poison to make a photograph,
also time, water and paper
but not always a camera with a lens—
just a small hole in the wall of a room
will do
if it's dark as an ether can
inside, then God's spy on earth
the promiscuous eye
enters and puts to sleep
time, water and paper.

In Old Barcelona

They didn't know it was him—
the old man in the street, hit by a tram
at the intersection of Gran Via
and Carrer de Bailén,
without a wallet or identification,
his stonemason's apron
covered in blood, his beard flecked
with concrete chips, his face dotted
with bits of colored stone
and broken bottles from the street.
He lingered two days
while broken ribs bent into his lung
and was buried behind his cathedral,
its spires shaped like cypress trees.
When the anarchists came
they blew up his models and burned
his blueprints, and opened the grave
of his benefactor, scattering a rich man's
bones like dice, until more than half were lost
in the vineyards of Catalonia.
Because Gaudi worked with his hands
they forgave his piety and left him alone;
of Lorca, that sodomite
not even a wrist bone remains
not even an empty grave.

DR. WILLIAMS DELIVERS A BABY

Dr. Williams was making his rounds:
one dilapidated house, then another,
powdered oxygen on the aluminum siding,
brown shingles on the roofs.
In between visits, he'd sit in his car
a notebook on his lap and arrange words—
instruments on a surgical tray—
uterine sounds blunt as tire-irons,
scalpels sharper than paper.
Often a cry from within the house
would bring him running past its yard,
past a tomato plant or wheelbarrow or red hen,
things he took in as he sprang
up the porch steps, hoping the family
was already in the parlor, had put the kettle on,
had found clean towels and disinfectant
to swab the wound or welcome the crowning head.
He put down his old-fashioned doctor's bag,
a satchel peaked like a dormer at both ends,
his initials stamped in gold, long ago faded,
and took off his wool overcoat. Tonight,
he noted the burdened book shelves,
responsible chair, the goose-necked reading lamp,
the desk loaded with papers, writing tools
and a folding pince-nez: the father
was a professor or writer of some degree,
who could afford both coal and electric.
He suspected they were Jewish, the mother
of German ancestry, the father Sephardic—
but had no reason to know. In truth
he had only a cursory familiarity with their tribe
and knew no Hebrew. But the mother's cry?

Soon, it was going to be soon. He timed her pain
until a dark spot between her labia grew
and it was time to prep and drape her;
then he encouraged the head with a gloved hand
turned the shoulders and delivered the rest.
Dr. Williams told the father it looked like a writer,
this noisy boy, vigorous and exploring.
They would name him Allen.

What He Must Have Been Thinking

"Witnesses say that the men aboard the dinghy were standing erect
at the moment of the blast, as if in some kind of salute."
Fouad Ajami, NYT, 10-17-00

He thought it was just a step through a door
and out to another world, his hand off
the trigger, would feed himself figs as he sat
in the shadow of a vine, climbing up
a yellow wall his great uncle had once owned
in Jaffo. He was pretty sure the old
wooden key they gave him still fit the door.
In a moment, he was inside their house
could see lamb and wine on the table,
just as they left it fifty years ago,
and there was his girl—unveiled, looking
directly at him, her skin disappearing
as she danced, translucent
like his silk-covered hand reaching for a gun.
He felt the sea swell off the beach of Haifa
then roll against the skiff in Aden's harbor.
The sun struck the Cole like iron on a stove,
and his spine straightened—he would meet
God erect, not as when he knelt in a mosque,
its blue and white tiles overhead.
Years ago, his cousin drove a loaded truck,
made his way through bunkers in Beirut,
as deliberate as a mailman, a casual smile
on his lips and killed two hundred and forty-one
marines and sailors. Did his father know this?
Another moment passed—then a flash
and on the other side of time
he found nothing existed except eternity;

it swept towards him like a sonic boom.
He flew so fast he missed the seventeen souls
flying in the same direction. Missed the shards
of smoking metal, missed the pig smell of flesh
fired into the air. Missed the sound of his death
when his head blew off
moments before he was born.

September Sonnet

Auden was right—our buildings grope
the sky for certainty but are dumb
and blind. In the fierce limbus of my eye
the plummeting birds burn still,
asbestos rains and twisted steel
falls in a broth of jet fuel,
cable wrap and mineral dust;
it bathes the snouts of corpse-hunting
dogs and spatters our helmeted Nimrods.
Who stoked these fires while we slept?
Who blew on the embers
filling September with regret,
and who will be consoled if irony dies
a thousand deaths? Not you or I.

Notes On First Hearing
Alkan's Funeral March

It seemed a peculiar thing to do—
a funeral march on the death of a parrot.
Alkan, a piano prodigy and intermittent hermit,
was known to be crabby and over wrought.
When Chopin died in 1849, Alkan withdrew
from giving concerts and locked himself up
in a two-story apartment, large enough
so he could play his pédalier, a grotesque
chimera of organ pedal board and grand piano,
without disturbing his neighbors.
He was not seen in public again
for twenty-five years. Perhaps the parrot
was his sole companion, the only one
who could stand the noise.
(No need to imply the relationship was odd
in other ways, and his grief commensurate
with his loss.) Of course, the death of composers
is better known than the deaths of their pets.
Alkan's own is even more famous than all
but a few, including Gershwin's brain tumor,
misdiagnosed as a type of neurosis,
and Lully's death by gangrene of his great toe
three months after he'd stabbed himself
with a sharply pointed walking stick
while vigorously conducting an opera.
In 1888, Charles Francois Alkan killed himself
when a complete set of the Talmud fell on his head;
death by knowledge was appropriately rewarded
by burial in Montmartre on April Fools' day.
The obituary said "it was necessary for him to die
in order to suspect his existence."

Notice In *The Times*

So long as he's alive
the world rolls under the long thrust of his heel.
When he dies, the notice in the *Times*
reburies one of his wives with him,
spends half his space on an old rumor,
no notice that he was the black crow
of poetry, his bright eye pierced
with the countryside
his voice like a rabbit snare
tricked by the charm of repetition.

His spondees were right; of course
everything dies, as did two of his wives
and children, bored by the farm in Devon where
smoke burned his sermons into the skies
and the curlew flew
and the hedgerows hid great gouts of blood
and charred bone, (though not from him)
until overwhelmed by his theme
he lay down to sleep
with fox, crow and sheep,
not noticed in the *Times*.

Be Not Afraid

When attacked by an anaconda
a government memorandum advises
do not run, it's faster than you are,
just lie on the ground with your chin tucked in,
legs together, hands at the sides
and be not afraid.

Stay very still while it crawls all over you
even though it weighs 3 to 400 pounds
and its skin might be called cool and slimy.
Eventually it will settle its mouth
at your feet—but there's no need to panic.

At first, it will suck on your toes
like a green lover, then ingest your ankles
gradually working its way up to your shins;
when it's ready to swallow your knees
prepare for action:

slowly reach around its head, swaying
at your waist and grab your knife, drive
it through the top of its mouth
and into its brain, ignore the red
porridge pouring out,
and cut its head off at the upper jaw

and calm yourself. Oh yes,
you did remember to carry a knife
didn't you? Make sure
that it's long enough and very sharp
with a serrated blade and back leaning teeth
that rip and won't let go, just like
a serpent's tooth and don't be afraid.

Small Bones

In my hand an opera sings:
navicular and lunate speak of a boat drifting too close
to a moon, hamate and capitate of the hook
that will seek the performer's head
if he sings off-key, and like a modern staging
of Antigone, the rest of my wrist bones
are abstract props, pisiform, triquetrum,
trapezoid and trapezius, geometric shapes
against which the songs of my fingers lean,
metacarpals and phalanges drumming
my noises, tapping my rhythms, disguising my rage.
I imagine at the end of this musical play
the entire cast will close in a fit or spasm,
before fisting the earth with their gelatin nails.

GEORGE STEVENS MAKES A MOVIE

You think his love of grand guignol began
with Monty Clift biting the lips off of Liz
or James Dean burning up those Texas hills
like old celluloid exploding in a can?
You think he didn't know just what Ike meant
when he said 'hey George, they'll tell lies about
what happened here, so let's make a film
too terrible to see'? How could he not be bent
to his work, recording mounds of breathing
corpses, still steaming with the aroma of gas?
From March to May, they freed the ghosts—
not a few fluttered like birds and passed.
Well before *Giant*, Stevens had been blooded
making a movie in which nothing moved.

BACK TO THE FUTURE

my uncle's nose peers above the sheets,
the extreme outpost of his face (cf:
The Devil's Dictionary, by Ambrose Bierce),
curves gently down like a sparrow's beak,
intuits nothing that's coming at him,
has never known the aroma of the infinite,
but points at me like a finger, 'you're next'.
On the instep of his arm, bluish numbers
from the 40's turn slightly green, blanch
with each remaining breath. No outlook
left, he can't prop up on an elbow,
can't pierce the one hospital window
in his room, shuttered against Long Island,
gray and smug. In a Jewish hospital
filled with black faces, he calls me Joshua,
my son's name, confuses my wife
with my mother. We're all mixed up—
three generations stuck in his brain's blender
starved for electricity. Today, invisible clumps
of cells clot his veins, turn his guts melanotic.
Fifty years ago, he made a magical escape,
turned a Houdini, but now his tricks are stale:
where is your laugh, dear uncle, your crooked
crossbeak smile, and after your pledge,
your glass of ginger ale, your ersatz scotch and soda?
Your pj's are too pale, no yellow twist of silk
in your breast pocket, no sash at your hip;
what would the guys on Seventh Avenue say
in their tasseled loafers and pressed trousers?
Not one has come to see your nose today,
its precipice hanging on a timberline, tracing
the distance between a grimace and a grin.

The Unlabeled Dead

My father's death may well surround me
with inscrutable photographs,
cousins and aunts standing in rows,
their scarf-covered heads
sepia-toned,
and uncles lost forever to the gentiles—
some of the unlabeled dead
of Kosice and Bratislava.

Here's my mother in a prewar pose—
in a pink and rose ballerina's dress,
her chin en point on her fingers,
as much a coquette at twelve

as she will ever be.
And my father in uniform, already balding,
sometimes with mustache, sometimes not,
he who was also an engineer and a scholar,

who was almost a rabbi,
he who saved himself in the sewers of Prague,
and who rescued these photographs more fireproof than flesh;
may he never tell me their meaning.

KATYA'S GREAT ROMANCE

1.

At the end of the war, my mother Edith lay down in an alley too narrow for tanks,
warmed by the carcass of a dead horse; her documents said she was Katya

and this is what she did: she lived alone, went to church and crossed herself
as often as necessary. She made thermos bottles in a factory.

2.

Grandma's maid, who used to go with her to a park near the big house in Nižný
Hrabovec, was named Kitty. Late in the day, Kitty would close the silk bonnet

of her carriage to keep the sun from tanning Edith black as a gypsy.
Sometimes, Katya brought her dates along and the three of them would stroll

beneath the plane trees. When Edith was five, a man with a moustache,
who liked to ride horses, appeared. He could lift her like a loaf of bread

from the perambulator with his farm strong hands. At the side of her dead horse,
she thought "I'll never see him again", so she dreamt of bread—

not her ballerina's dress or jester's hat, not even her violin, but something to eat
in that alley as cold as the brickyard in Kosice, where she saw her parents selected

3.

for Auschwitz. While the adults compliantly left for the trains, thinking it
only a necessary humiliation, Edith became a milk maid, holding out

her empty milk can, feeding the forced laborers and blessing those
who pretended to drink. Was it Marie Antoinette they last saw or Little Bo Peep

4.

before she slowly drifted away and walked across the border to Budapest?
After the war, my Father looked for grandma and her maid, and forgot about

the little daughter in the stroller, the one who opened the door to him now,
          her arms
unmarked, unafraid. At first he failed to recognize who stood there in the
          doorway,

all grown up at seventeen: she who was Miriam in Hebrew, the sister of Aaron
and Moses, also Edith the Jewess and Katya the maid. But my mother knew

it was the man who had pushed her carriage in the park. And because the dead
          do not
travel or read books or speak the unspeakable, she went with him to America.

THE PASSAGE

It was a dream I had—
taking the last train out from Prague,
my father-in-law's gold pocket watch smuggled
through the window by a cousin at the station,
my bag freighted by the bronze statuette of a naked lady
holding a wolf's head while she stands
on two gears enmeshed on a marble base.
No jewels, cash, or silver candlesticks,
only the symbol of the Skoda Works.
From Holland to England to America, the trip took a month
and though the ocean crossing was the least part,
my son was afraid.

> *I don't remember anything on the boat except the wading pool*
> *for children, a small pond traveling across a great lake*
> *and the storm.*

It began to rain, the wind pushed the ship
from side to side, no longer making way across the Atlantic, it pitched
up and down and he began to cry, afraid the engines would stop
and he would be stuck part way between the known
and what was to come.
I held him in my lap, more like a good mother than a man
and told him about the elephant I had seen astern,
its long legs long enough to reach the bottom of the ocean,
its heavy brow pushing us across the sea
until my son slept through the night.

> *I still wake up to check the pumps on my boat;*
> *I still don't trust any machine that's blood dry*
> *in its bones. I still believe in that elephant—*
> *a father never lies.*

WRESTLING IN BROOKLYN

My father must be the oldest wrestling fan
in the world; at ninety, he thinks
it's an honest game, not acting, not a fix,
that beneath their masks and makeup,
Greek and Roman athletes grapple
with the fates. He came to America
after the last good war and couldn't see
the distinction. I was nine when we got
our twelve inch Dumont
and even then I knew they were geeks:
white hats like Bruno Sammartino
or Argentina Rocca with his hairy legs;
bad guys like Killer Kowalski,
(who could paralyze you
with just two fingers) or Gorgeous George
and his platinum curls. Most of all
there was Haystack Calhoun,
four hundred pounds of mean in blue overalls;
he wore a horseshoe around his neck
and used it to bash in the foreheads of opponents.
The truest test of faith was waiting for Rocca
to manage an escape from beneath
that enormous press of flesh, my Father
cheering good in its triumph over evil, me laughing
at his trusting kindness—got Mother mad
in the kitchen; she'd yell for me to tone it down
but my sarcasm never managed to spoil
his simple pleasures; he knew it was safe
to be foolish in Brooklyn.

The Year The Dodgers Won The Pennant

One of these streets led us out of Brooklyn—
I could see it from my sixth floor window
as I peered down into a brick courtyard we called the "alley"
surrounded by a horseshoe of garages
faces covered with green doors and black latches
iron and wood, as if there were horse drawn
carriages parked inside instead of Bel Airs & Pontiacs.
We played stickball in the alley and touch football
on the street until a side view mirror was bent by
a shoulder making an extra yard and I thought
they'd catch us. Now and then, my mother looked down
from the sixth floor like Thor in a dress
and shouted at boys taunting me as I stumbled
afraid of turning my palsied ankle on a manhole
cover. In my room we took turns playing the girl,
two boys with acne and bad breath. We sat
on the front steps where gray dirt surrounded
the lone tree or up on the tar and gravel roof
where you snapped galvanized antennas off
in your hand and traced ribbon wire cables
over the building's edge until we felt them connect
and talked about books none of our friends had read.
And when it was really hot we'd sit on the iron steps
debating Poe and Whitman; in the cool shadows
of that alley, it felt like a life, even then.

THIS IS THE HAND

My father's hand, the old engineer
of his blueprints, trained
in European cursive
to flourish and be clear,
doesn't betray its age
by spidery indecision or tremor
but discloses by its shapeliness
and Jeffersonian character,
a means fitted to a temper
and a time long gone
when writing a letter to your son,
especially, was an event.

He sometimes wrote on bonded
paper, its watermark wire-laid,
its handmade pulp crisped
like parchment; of this
a few sheets remain
in a drawer that smells
of lemon oil, almonds, and wood:
the odor of our Bensonhurst
synagogue, where my head perfumed
in his side, listens as he prays,
and watches his fingers coil the fringes
of his shawl, ashamed of his rage.

My father's hand had a history—
in its slashing t's
and long-looped y's
you can read a man with enough energy
to throw a punch at an anti-Semite
in a prison camp,

but seeing fear, couldn't strike.
He once raised it against me
but his hand shrank back
like God before Nineveh
sorrowed by its possible destruction.

OUR SON DISCOVERS PANTYHOSE

Think of all the generations that missed the mystery
of pantyhose, the sheer idiocy of wrapping up
that which becomes unwrapped each evening,
of warming the cold perfection of ankles,
calves and thighs, of fastening a crotch to catch
the gifts of blood and cum, adding its slippery feel
to limbs and sex entwined like nucleic acids
donated to the child, who before he becomes
himself, stretches the unbranched chains of Lycra
and nylon almost to their breaking point,
then hides his five year old face in a nest
of woven fibers with the same crooked smile
you smiled the night we reclined to make him.

THE ICE HOUSE

Later, in our yearbook, they caption a photo of George,
his mouth gaping open as if to say
'we're going to carry what up from where?',
that first day of class two or three of us at a time lift
bodies onto a fireman's stretcher, and carry the corpses
out of a late nineteenth century red brick Victorian
across a small courtyard and up a short flight of stairs
into the anatomy lab next door. The dead weigh more
than we do, fresh from the ice house they're heavier still,
hands at their sides, standing attention in repose,
their clay-colored faces flat as cardboard, eyes closed
lips pursed, holding in the separate secrets
of their final moments, the fleeing of their souls.
Because of a shortage in donations, it's four to a body.
Over the next weeks and months, nerves and tendons
come up to greet the ministrations of our knives.
We give them names before we flay (in order)
their extremities, belly, heart and head, and leave nothing
much behind except attachments to bone, the black
tongue and the brain in its casement. Not all of us
are equally deft—you can already tell who the future
surgeons are and who the psychoanalysts. We make
the usual jokes about girls who study late and fall asleep
over the bodies, but in general these dead get a modicum
of respect not accorded them in life.
They're the first people we learn to read like books,
exemplars of the future and texts off the street.

THE NEW MAN

They say there's nothing new under the sun
but I found him in the steam room at the gym
today, his skin covered with tattooed snakes,
his left nipple pierced, a pair of birthstones
in each ear and a ring in the foreskin of his penis.
He smelled beyond the normal odor of the gym
and when he stretched his legs before him,
I saw a jeweled eye imbedded in a snake coil
on his outer thigh and grinned how queer
a man this was (gay or sad I couldn't tell)
who would use such attachments during sex.
But how?—is the question I'd love to ask
without a desire to hear the answer.
All the same, there's no place else to put
my eyes so I watch him coil and uncoil
his arm, its adornment a watercolor, supple
like paper money, etched in blue, red
and green, and it makes me think of Blake—
not his poems but his engravings:
the famous ones of Newton's muscles stripped
to do trigonometry and God's flowing mane,
spread wing-like over the oceans.
I wipe my humid eyes with a towel from my lap
and watch a self-created man, no god
or science has touched, ignore me,
his private thoughts turned public acts
in this glass enclosure. His warning is silent
and self-contained; I am the first to leave.

The Block, 1952

Despite her smeared lipstick, I think she's a matron
who hates to be immobilized even for a little while;
her aching back pains with frustration.
Not that she'd complain—in the past few months
alone, three lady friends have died of cancer
but she smiles and says she's had a good life:
four children, an equal number of husbands,
and all those trips up north when vaudeville
was king just so Blaze Starr could follow the circuit south;
a stripper's code of honor, headliners didn't compete.
"When Blaze first worked the Block, she was flat
as a little girl. But after she got injected,
we all went up to touch her chest—her breasts
were so hard with plastic that when she lay down,
they sat up like teacups!" She laughs
and circles her hands like tassels,
dozens of rings and bracelets tinkling,
then takes a moment to smooth her hair, still streaked
with henna and big like Baltimore in 1952.
She played all the best places: the Trocadero,
the Oasis and the Two O'clock Club (where Blaze
was the star), when the Block was really the block
and the White Castle wasn't a burger joint.
In those days, a girl felt safe; the cops hung out
at Fayette and Fallsway, waiting for their payoffs.
She remembers the sitters who drank in the afternoon,
shy men who never looked up at the girls,
and every shortstop and working stiff
whoever fell in love with her. She grimaces
and shifts position. She hopes it's a disc,
that makes her leg go numb whenever she tries
to dance with her grandchildren, and not a tumor,
something I can fix. I lift her leg up until she cries;
the wrinkled satchel of her life overflows in my hand.

THE BARGELLO

It's not what they meant, let me tell you,
when they set up Donatello among the wild beasts
gave him a cold chisel, a gouge
and a rasp to chew the marble away
from the hollow in the block,
thick tools to chase the hairs in his David
from the veins in ten tons of rock,
dragged by mules and men from a quarry
far away from Florence.
They brought it to him on rollers,
like a tomb for a pharaoh—see
what you can do with this—and he began
to chip away the stone in Goliath's forehead
and polish it brown over many months
until it stood out in the open, proud
like a third eye swollen and bruised
or a great emerald in the mind.
No, it's not what they wanted
but it's what they got;
and they built a museum to house it and contain
this mighty eructation of tearing away.

TITIAN'S LAST PAINTING

I don't wonder Titian placed his own face
on the satyr hung by his heels
and flayed by Apollo;
don't wonder at all a small dog laps
the puddle of blood collecting
beneath Marsyas's body—he
was probably old and tired of pressing
his thoughts on those who could still
walk away, not bound as he was
upside down, listening to his brain
nattering on about the inconvenience
of lapsing into a coma brought on
by his rival's god-like force and in-
consideration. He thought 'they'll still play
the flute after I'm gone and lick
the paint left behind like a pheromone
or whatever that little dog is used to
sniffing, not flesh shaved in strips
from bone and hanging like my sex did
when sex and music mattered more than life.'

THE ROKEBY VENUS

She turns her back on us.
Not merely a metaphor
but a woman Velázquez really knew,
with the same long curve

to the line of her back that you
have, ending in dimples paired at the spine,
where her flesh is smooth and pink as pearls dissolved
in milk.

No imaginary madrileña,
but the mistress of a marquis, Gaspar de Haro,
who mounted her likeness
on the ceiling of his secret room in Madrid,

her face blurred in the mirror
held by a perfect cherub,
so that his wife
would not know her name and could not see it.

Why also turn away?
Was it shame or some debt she felt
was owed the old man or had she guessed
what held the gaze of her painter?

Like him, I almost can't bear to breathe
before this great medallion of creamy flesh,
before the woman who beckoned
as he nailed her to the canvas.

Did he rationalize what he couldn't deny
and is that why he painted her
from behind, turning her back just in time
as if to say goodbye?

STUBBS NOT SEEN

Attacked by a lion, the chestnut stallion
rises on pewter hooves, eyes lit
by a stripe of crimson lightning,
his breath a gray blast across the room
in which we stand astonished at his fear
and the green calm in which the cat resides
crouched in a corner of the canvas.
Stubbs got each articulation right—
each joint moves as it once did hoisted
on his block and tackle, specimens lifted
up into the barn air, and flayed in layers
stripped of skin and hair, muscle and bone.
Hour after hour, in the mad heave of the pulley
He avenges their deaths, not his own.

EIGHT EAKINS PORTRAITS

I-THE PAIR-OARED SHELL (1872)

It's painting as arithmetic—
the shadows fall this many squares to the right
or left, so you can tell the exact time (7:20 PM)
and date (May 28th or July 27th) he drew them:
John Biglin and his brother Barney, dun-colored
scarves tied like do-rags to their heads, blue and red
parts of a contraption whose abdomen,
a pared down shell of varnished cedar, glides
like a water-bug, its eight legs made of arms
and oars pulled together by a blithe pair of acrobats
on the Schuylkill River, until the scull and its track
pass the far truss of the railroad bridge and the sun
sets. Eakins often pulled an oar himself when not
engineering his paint to bear the full stress.

II-THE GROSS CLINIC (1875)

Back from Paris and already 30, Eakins wished to make
a splash. In his great medical machine, Samuel David Gross
of Jefferson College stands as brown as an Amsterdam brick.
Behind his shining brow, we watch his brain think
can even hear it speak. "Look", he says to the cartoon heads
ranked in rows above him, "I'm reality, this case
nothing else", the bright point of his knife balanced nicely
in a bloody hand. Some assistant holds the boy's legs, thinly clad
in gray socks, a second retracts the wound, a third probes
the incision for pus, another chloroforms the face.

To our left, the mother averts her eyes from a scene so gross
it makes a New York critic gag, its pyramid of shapes placed
as dispassionately as an anatomical demonstration
or a tower artfully composed of Cambodian skulls.

III-THE SWIMMING HOLE (1883-1885)

Early in his teaching career, Eakins made plaster casts
of anatomical dissections, legs, arms and backs,
also photographs of trotting horses and men
as they tumbled into the darkness. He often drew
his models naked, their faces masked, a shadow's flame
behind their heads. Asked to "resign" three times
for letting women sketch nudes of both sexes,
he paints a snap of four boys on a rock,
poses one like The Dying Gaul, another like Pan.
To our right, a diver and his spray, at left a man
glistened with wet holds to a ledge, the other arm bent
at a paddling dog. And just as he planned
we notice Eakins last—in the bottom corner, bearded
swimming strongly as he can to where his divided self waits.

IV-PORTRAIT OF WALT WHITMAN (1887-1888)

You see me now as the fierce friend of my final years
saw me; though he painted me resting, I'm not at rest
my brain whirls with continents. My eyes are open,
though death is limned in me like sweet drunkenness
and my cheeks remain ruddy. Around my head
and lips the gray hairs billow like wisps of smoke
or a final breath. On my shoulder, a flat collar flares
a white epaulet—none owned by Falstaff nor painted

by Hals was ever finer though I'm hardly a gay toper
like them. Sorely vexed when first we met, he wrote
"My honors are misunderstanding, persecution and neglect,
enhanced because unsought". I think he caught me dreaming
of his resignation and bitterness; I never liked this likeness
much (not that I told him).

V-MISS AMELIA Van BUREN (1891)

Only in her twenties when she was painted
this way, "Minnie's" pensive air and gray hair
make her look much older than she was. The pink
Victorian dress doesn't much flatter her either
but Eakins was once her teacher and didn't need to.
You can almost see each stitch in the print
of her crinoline apron, watch the blue buds climb
over the shadowed folds in her lap, feel the heft
of a fan lying cross-wise in the rills. She looks away
to our left, eyes up, head at rest on a loosely fisted hand.
She's not depressed, exactly, though her tight lips speak
of regret, some lost child, perhaps, a friend
or lover who disappointed, a loss of possibilities revealed
by a flash of thigh in a class for which he lost his job.

VI-PORTRAIT OF PROF. HENRY A. ROWLAND (1897)

The painting alone is more than good enough, the buzz
of thought rising upright in a chair. Rowland sits
like a totem with a straight blade nose
and high forehead, his hands holding a diffraction grating
of ruled steel from which an entire rainbow spills
to break the dark illumination of his laboratory.

In the background, Tom Schneider, his legs hidden
by the ruling machine, worships like a devil's assistant.
Add to all this the gilt frame incised by the artist and it goes
over the top—four cedar planks Eakins carved with equations
and ratios, important constants and the proportionate rule
of the spectrophotometer. That same year, Gauguin cuts
his door posts in Tahiti, gouges them with the visage of his own
god but never wraps them around a face like this icon does.

VII-PORTRAIT OF MRS.THOMAS EAKINS (1899)

She looks too sad to love him, can't forgive his need
to get the light right on her chin, can't rejoice how his
obsession has temporarily pushed aside the wish
to photograph men and boys, can't forget his river
of debt and discouragement, or his cold disdain
for imprecision. He was forty when they wed.
Whitman said he was "a force of nature",
not a painter, but she tried to contain him like a valley
cradles a storm. They made no children in a life
hidden by facts—was she barren or had he lost interest
in her biology? He loved women like cats,
they were his familiars; none of his men crack
with this much emotion
or share his evident disappointment in the future.

VIII-SELF-PORTRAIT (1902)

True to himself in every respect,
it's more than photographic: worn and tired,
brows knit with distress, he stares beyond us
into the far distance, his mouth drawn down,

lips set for a single breath, his eyes alert but barely
wet in a shabby bow tie, jacket and vest,
his beard flecked with winter's colors. Science
is dispassionate and free of flattery. But close to the end,
he gave himself to the tenderness he once reserved
for his lady sitters, cousins and in-laws who never guessed
what potted well of bitterness he drew from.
"It's all right", I said, as if to calm his autumnal face
in a Philadelphia museum, "you're a big name now
and a man may see himself dead or alive in any order."

GAUGUIN'S HAND

His left, upright in the photograph,
is seen through a gray fog
as if in Brittany, the Marquesas or Tahiti,
its fifth finger slightly spread
from the others
like a carved totem, a phallus,
or the upraised arm of St. Jerome
in a Leonardo.
The fourth bears a narrow band
discarded two years later
despite a wife and children.
The second, a half head shorter than the third,
is pressed as closely as a lover with its neighbor
and his thumb makes with them
a checkmark in reverse
or the notation of a gull at sea,
so that above this vee
his fugitive eye hangs
like a saint's might— peeling from a fresco
and as fanatically clear.
Is it Gauguin or Leclerc
who presents this disconnected hand to us,
its mysterious flesh ourselves
wishing to cast spells or throw clay?

LOOKING AT KLINE

Looking at Kline
is like entering the jaws of a whale—
the baleen hanging down every which way,
the elevator cage,
the ride down his insides
back to the Pennsylvania hills
to the coal mines,
to the white strips of ash
smoldering on the hillside after the lightning strikes.
Back, back to the trestles
and the towns
and the trains he named them for—
"Diamond" and "Chief" and "Mahoning";
back to the towers east of Tenth street
painted white and black,
tensioned like steel bands,
like prison bars and slack air,
like the soot and the flare of a sodium lamp
burning in the hand of Ahab.

Blue: Barnett Newman's *Ulysses*, 1952

A vertical slab of two blues rises
like a cut section of sky,
cloudless, serene, ready to topple our eyes
with a fluorescent, foamless wave.
The painting wears its pretentious name
like a flag, Newman as Homeric voyager
tacking his standard to a wall in Ilium,
too tall for me or any mere Adam
to scale or look for a hand hold.
By actual survey, blue's the world's favorite
color (except in Turkey where it's green)
and the blues is what he listened to
as he painted in monocle and vest.
He spent more time looking at *Ulysses*,
sitting on a canvas seat, keeping his suit
clean, than actually using a brush
or roller to paint its balance and purity.
He studied Kabala and once ran for mayor
as an anarchist, before he found his true style
and métier, hectoring others to do the same.
He was famous for not showing enough
but withheld nothing. He knew
what was blue and what was not.

DOUBLE ORANGE CAR CRASH

It's a lot like deciphering the symbols
in a Breughel; who are these smiling faces?
In a hundred years, I bet no one will hang
Andy's vanity portraits of starlets,
captains of commerce,
or society matrons in a museum,
each painted at forty thousand dollars a pop,
because no one will know their names,
just his.
They might not even hang our immortal
ephemera, those Coke bottles, dollar signs
and faux boxes of Del Monte peaches
because he wasn't the first to press ink
through a screen or worship the transitory.
So not too much will last of his hipness
except a cool stare and his silver fright wig
in that cheap polaroid, silent and coy
about what he meant.
I know he loved their pure desperation,
that's what unites them, Liz and Jackie,
Elvis and Marilyn, with the bodies thrown
in a tree, the man jumping out of a building,
the head crushed by an orange and black
car wreck,
the skulls, guns and switchblades,
the red electric chairs and the self-portraits
with surgical scars.
Oh they'll remember Andy, all right
like Breughel, like Bosch, our own Mr. Death.

DECONSTRUCTING ABSTRACTION:
A JOAN MITCHELL PAINTING

I was edging into middle age
the day my son found a marigold
in the corner of an abstraction,
putting in what the artist had taken
such care to take out, his eye
divining an image in a spot of yellow paint,
and felt some pride at his finding out
what occult wisdom meant, a decoding
of sense from sense, of signs
embedded in traces.
He was young then and Joan already dead—
her last years spent with a cancer's
pincers at her throat, the smell of smoke
on her Parisian scarf, a shot glass
in her hand—the common memory
of friends who told me sick or not
she was a handful, angry and elegant
until the end. My own eye went beyond the flower
to a formless scarf of blue, its smear
a recollection of Lake Michigan,
where her mother made Joan skate
like a champion.
It was early on when she drew this spinning hand
grenade of dark earth at the bottom edge
of the canvas, pulling its pin
to anchor the drip
of black piss or rain.
We both saw she had already changed
her pirouette, had to.

RED: THE COLOR THAT ADVANCES

When you try to make a point, they always say
'who are we to judge?' as if it weren't
a question but a fact that everything in the world's
of equal value. But the brain is built to compare
and can't see red unless there's a green nearby,
can't know comfort without some painful contrast.
Cezanne intuitively knew how the brain sees red,
knew the eye was his touch extended,
that a green cloth and blue salver made
the apple red, that it takes two colors
to make a parade or procession.
In a bowl of painted fruit
red is the color that advances.

In making your portrait, a painter gloved and masked
grinds pigments or buys poisons,
the arsenic sulfide that apes cinnabar
and smells like almonds in your hair
or boils quicklime and sulfur
in an alembic glass. He will ask me
if your cheeks are cherry red
like carbon monoxide, and I will answer,
there's no red without risk, thinking of
the coal tar in your carmine lips, feeling it
own the heat of its making, just like love.
In a bowl of painted fruit
red is the color that advances.

LOVE IN THE AGE OF MECHANICAL REPRODUCTION

She stands beside the bed naked,
a Mickey Mouse phone in her hand,
no longer an abstraction,
or a concept like salvation,
but an image stronger than memory:
her pale flesh, the left arm diagonal
on her breast, one hand modestly drawn
between her legs, her lips caught
half way between a smile
and the "oh" of surprise
at my camera flash.
Long after she's gone,
this photo is all I've got left,
so I take it out
from its drawer, uncurl the edges
and center it on a flat bed
scanner. Instantly,
she turns into silicon,
her nipples become pixels,
her bright hair any color I wish.
A secret part of my jelly wet brain
has been transferred to a machine
but I've never called this jpeg up—
why would I dare? I might make her
somehow different or myself the same.

MISSING YOU, I NOTICE THINGS

Down Michigan Avenue
a pair of stiffened workman's gloves
stand on a stone bench in Grant park,
their fingers bent
grappling with the sky.
Behind the bench
their owner sleeps
out of sight
of lovers, their world still wrapped
in envy's colors,
insensible to the disembodied few.
And fifty yards away
the lions' (otherwise also green)
tails remain bronze colored,
rubbed smooth
by children's fingers
and I notice that even their testicles
are green and flat like the cow skull reliefs
on the nearby planters
which, excepting their Egyptian garlands
echo O'Keeffe's jewel box paintings inside
the Art Institute.
Missing you, I notice things,
jot down points on a map,
march along Michigan Ave in September,
ornamenting it with your eyes.

ROMANTIC ORGAN

In daylight, I don't know the heart at all.
I have seen it in a jar, each muscle fiber matted
by formaldehyde
submerged in the gray-green light, held to the window,
like a tuberous plant among the lilies.
I have held it in my hand while it rested
between penultimate beats
and plunged a finger through its sucking
valves while life swirled red and frantic.
I have seen its chambers magnified many fold
by electrons and invoked in prayer.
I have seen it on the point of a maniac's knife
and punctured by a bullet; in the eyes
of a friend's wife or my own children
I have seen it broken but have never known it
like an Aztec might holding it up to the sun.
Only you have seen the one I carry like lead
inside me;
I don't know the daylight heart at all.

THE OFFERING

I lay down an unsheathed blade
shined-up and hairless, newly demented
and felt a tingle, spine to spine
as a finger does touching the edge of a new book.
It was only a pile of stones,
not an altar, its warmth against my back
at dusk on the mountain top,
its heat searching my bones,
the faggots of wood
burning with a small pop and glow.
I was thinking cypress and pine would warm me up
but stayed cold and silent for hours, shivered
as I watched you build it up around me,
my mind wandering until I could see
their eyes in the darkness, forever lost
in the cities, in the desert, in the ovens
and felt my death might prevent it all
if you faltered and saved me.
But it was never up to just the two of us.
I'm sure you heard the ram thrashing
in the brambles when I did,
your-up raised hand shook with my fear
then a fluttering sound like wings came
and it was over—
who could know this act of kindness
would feel like such a blow?

SCENT

Afterwards, I smell you like hot butter rising
from my thighs,
my hand pollinated with your musk,
and the tack of your underclothes
spouts lavender and lilies of the valley
in my reptilian brain.
Furiously, I drive to my next stop
the last trace of your liquor in me
like ECT, like a tree struck down
in an electrical storm
kept twitching by the ozone
released around it,
every axon and dendrite
shaken in its spine
by the memory of you.
Oh, Proust knew why the ancients met eternity
surrounded by unguents and perfumed creams:
even the dead can dream
shaken by such a scent.

QUANTUM LOVE

If you open my little box-
shaped head, you'll see me
sitting there
like Schrödinger's cat
alive and dead at once.
It's a quantum world I'm told—
I'm here and not here,
love is a wave or a bullet.
When your radioactive look
kills me, it's just what science does—
it unwraps the fascination.
And what about the probability
that somewhere on a neutron star
Newton stands, periwinkles
at his feet?
Does he still believe
the waves are real,
even in a neutron sea,
or is he too distracted
by love, and either
doesn't know his place
or can't measure her velocity?

A Dream Of Jaguars

Last night I dreamed of jaguars—
their green eyes set with emeralds,
their bodies cut from gray stone,
crouching in the narrowing heat
of the chambers hidden atop the airless pyramid
of Chichén Itzá.

Last night I walked the ball court,
stood before a mural of one-eyed skulls,
stared at the immortal captain
who holds his opponent's severed head,
and thought about the end of this game—
were the gods fed by the vanquished
or did they drink the blood of the victor?

That same night, the sky sighted
by a dreaming astronomer, sprayed its light
through the hole in Chacmool's belly
and engraved on green stone
the diving god and the flying serpent,
the jaguar of the emerald eye,
the several and singular gods of the Yucatan
who smile down on me
with your smile,
and drew my spirit toward a stone lintel
where I placed my hand against the red print
a priest had left
hundreds of years before
and found that it still fit.

When I awaken upon your breast
the green corn stands abashed,
the stench of a great cat in the jungle
flutters birds upon the frets of trees,
and the jungle recovers its bounty.
In the delirium I share with you
the jaguar is dreaming of me.

This Is Not A Rehearsal

A candy striper steps aboard
a crowded elevator, conveying today's ort
of philosophy on a white metallic button
pinned to her breast. We both see it—
the black letters say
"This Is Not a Rehearsal"; I sense
an urgency not proclaimed by Aristotle,
and touch, in a surreptitious way,
the inside of your arm, where a spot
between wrist and elbow
feels as warm as your pink genital flesh does.
It's the first next day and thoughts of us
together still bring twinges
as patients get off
and doctors on at each stop.
As good a Cartesian as you,
the aroma of sweat, raw silk
and lavender on my fingertips
does it for me; for five straight floors
our scent mixes with street odors
and ascends in my brain
like a Madeleine dipped in tea.
The crowd thins out, the girl with the button
has left, a nurse steps off with a tray, suddenly
it's our stop and I must let go of your arm
to watch the crisp blue edge
of your dress walk out just ahead
in the unconscious light of day.

THE GRAY CAT

A Persian cat sits at the window
and watches the snow fall. He's seen all this
before: the shaking leaves, the snow plow
slowly painting geometric tracks down
our street, the gray squirrel who bends
the maple branches that bat our kitchen walls.
I've read that simple movement excites him,
that the cells in his brain fire each time
a sharp-edged bar crosses the frontier
of a receptive field. I know how the pump
of adrenalin makes his eyes grow wild
with the possibility of game.
But I watch his tail for hours and know
I'm wrong. It flicks, a slow metronome,
as if watching snow fall for almost an hour
were a problem in philosophy, the nature
of free will or the improbability of two flakes
superimposed on stone. I watch him pace
the sill, a small caged panther. Free,
he'd never keep his coat clean
out where the wild hare makes busy tracks
like cloverleafs. He'd miss our warm grates,
his dish of gruel, the place on my blanket
where he sleeps at night, his comfort,
his fate. How can he judge the value
of the exchange he's made? No mortgage
to pay, no children to feed; just blind hunger
that makes him jump at the darting light
my watch flashes on the wall,
his paws slapping at a moth-like emblem
of freedom or greed—
one I flick as often as I can.

MAGICAL THINKING

No concept of the world, no roof
no Dark Ages, no Renaissance;
the child cocks an eye at a hill
behind which mammoths play.
The earth is still, the sun moves
past a five foot mountain
and dogs hawk the morning news:
what the red ants told them
what the child hears,
stories exchanged at night
on the terraces of their hill
looking at the stars spill
into their crater,
where there is no fire,
before Kepler
before Copernicus, and after.

Daybreak in the garden standing
he makes a small stream a jungle
river and blades of grass
fall like giant's teeth,
the green stalks bend
the light he chases
as if nothing down the ages
were this gold, this warm.
He knows it all never happened
or it might again;
then he starts to roll slowly
towards the pea plants,
his mother calling after him—

Jack!

The Road To Machu Pichu

At five I read and never forgot
Ripley's most famous ad:
"a band of travelers froze to death
beneath a hot equatorial sun. Believe it or Not."
This was years before a plane crashed
in the Andes and the survivors made like Aztecs
eating the dead. Half a life later, I see for myself
how the road from Cusco to Machu Pichu ends
in Chillca, watch bromeliad grow
on the cliffs like grappling hooks, coral trees
blooming red in the Sacred Valley.
The train flies past swarms of yellow Scottish broom
and succulent agave in patches of red
impatiens and white orchids on the sloping rail bed.
Picking up speed, we hurry past
the unconscious faces of Incas who still dry bricks
in the sun, stake cows to the ridges, sow corn
in the ancient way. I note their disdain to see us
and remember how even the might of Spain
wasn't enough to claim their attention;
so why would the rush and noise of an engine
make their faces turn up from the agribusiness
of heaven? In their view, less than mountain spirits,
less than dead conquistadors, we and our train
are as transparent as silk leaves dressing the corn.

THE PHONE CALL

In the ether streaming
across a continent
an astral girl materializes

crawls through carbon and optical fiber
projects herself
as a hologram of desire

and tumesces
from a shy hello to warm wet sighs
as deliquescent as a dewdrop on buck thorn.

DROWNED RIVER AT THE LAZY MOON

for Thomas Lux

When the cows come down to drink
at Breden's Point, the boat slides
towards them, silent as a bearing
a jeweled wheel hovering in an old reliable watch.
They do not moo in the heat
but their ears twitch to hear the engine
just after I've shut it down, though
even brutes can't hear the past.
One and a half miles up river
Vera's onion domes and castellations appear;
in the thirties, she was almost a starlet
but married Greta Garbo's optometrist instead
and built herself an environment, White Sands
with its bamboo room,
ebony monkeys, elephant tusks
peacock chairs, leopard-skin barstools
and an old diving helmet made from brass.
It is in this room that she presides,
appears at sunset, thinking it flatters her
eighty years in a diaphanous dress,
sits near the piano man who plays
her blue-haired favorites
and sips champagne from a wide-mouthed glass.
On Solomons island, on a causeway built
of oyster shells, there's a nautical bookshop
where a sailor can find some courage
or a book of poems by a friend.
The day's so hot the sky's like soaped glass,
its wavering heat rises up
before my face and pulls me down.

Seven miles up the Pautuxent
it's Mozambique, Casablanca, the source of the Nile,
it's the end of the road
floating on a river.

Shooting The Moon With A Sextant

It can't be the same
sailing down the wide Patapsco
heading for the Bay, the same as

laundry or washing the car
or reaching the office at nine o'clock
on a Monday. It can't be the same

as calling your dad or waiting up
for the kids. It can't be the same
as writing checks or kissing your wife

on the cheek. It can't be the same
as cleaning the down spouts and gutters
or whisking the basement dry

with a broom. It can't be the same
as getting lunch meat from Eddie's
or shooting the moon

with a sextant. It can't be the same
at sea. There's no pharmacy
or hardware store at the corner;

there's no corner out there,
just the round ocean and flat sky
and sometimes a shitload of rain.

A Lamentation Of Swans

Like immortal cells growing in a dish
the alien swans multiply beyond our wish
for silent beauty. And the buried day rises as a dream—
how to kill the mute swans its theme,
one Tchaikovsky never penned,
is now debated in shore side bars and fens
by oystermen who lift their glasses
in sad farewell to black skimmers and underwater grasses;
they mourn the native tundra swan
and the least tern before it too is gone,
and if alien beauty must be trapped or shot
or poisoned, its nested eggs addled not
to hatch, they're willing to concede
how often beauty breeds dark necessity.

LANGUAGE AND THE BRAIN

"Imagination is intelligence with an erection"—Victor Hugo

Somewhere in the left hemisphere
of my brain, a monkey sits in a pile
of dictionaries, surrounded by old
typewriter keys, a word processor,
a thesaurus on a CD, a reef
of synonyms, a daisy chain of rhymes.
From this same location go out
the cables to my right arm, the nerve
that tracks to my heart and the half
of visual space to which my arm wires
the actions of my imagination.
You'd think the monkey in my brain
would get off my back, let me go
word blind looking at a painting,
let me see a woman's legs cross once
without the thought of making
some immortal gesture but no,
he knows the organ in which he sits
is as potent as any other
I'm afraid of losing, and when his pen
drills through my head, parsing cables
and trunk lines into syllables, I know
it's just the monkey begging to be fed
or else it's cursing, cursing, cursing.

FROM
THE ENEMY OF GOOD IS BETTER
(2011)

EUPHORIA

The world is round. From forty miles away
only the topmasts of ships appear headed
to the Bay Bridge, their hulls buried beneath
the curvature of gray water curling
along a short segment of latitude.

If you find the angle at which something
shrinks to nothing, you can get the distance.
A cross of wood, a length of twine
and soon enough the equator of existence
becomes a number as real as the belly
of an apple, a thing in the mind.

At sea you never doubt their rapture—
Archimedes predicting Newton,
Michelson Einstein—their excitement transparent
without fog of drug or spectacle.
And how big would a forest have to be
if each tree stood for a single neuron
in such a brain? A field as large as Manhattan
or Rhode Island, or all of Montana?
We calculate such vastness, we do not measure.
Here is the child's answer, stretching his arms
beyond his parents' grasp: *this big,* his body says.
No really, how big? This big. No. Bigger.

When The Boy Comes Back

I'm not too aware of him—he's shy
and it's easy for me to miss the sounds
and smells of his past:
the click of beads on an abacus
counting bushels of corn,
the cool swell of a glass doorknob
on a classroom door.

Or his hand warm from working the projector,
his ears come alive to the tick of the film strip
rising notch by notch, his alertness torn
between dust motes dancing above the fan
and the emulsion embossing the walls
with pictures of Mexico and Japan.

On such a night,
I hear him cranking the mimeograph drum,
mixing its violet smell
with the odor of oil in the rails of a slide rule—
an aroma as metallic as a brake in a machine shop,
where the boys bent els and smoothed their edges.

Drowsing off, he leaves me. And deeper asleep
even the clatter of typing with real type is gone:
the lunge of the carriage rising for a capital
and the little fists striking my words into place.

H*O*R*S*E

The games of childhood go on till dark,
everything precious enclosed like a garden
in the evening chill

of an empty schoolyard. The iron hoop
bends and springs back in the twilight,
clangs with the fiftieth shot

(a miss) thrown up by my wearying arms
rolled fat in a winter jacket.
I played H*O*R*S*E by myself a lot,

eyelids wet from squinting in the wind,
alternating shots with an absent friend
who'd grown impatient at how poorly I ran

on my one good leg, polio having starved
the left as thin as a cane. Swish
goes a two-handed set shot, swish a rare lay-up—

my elevation so flat my bad toe drags
on the ground, its sneaker squinching.
I move clockwise, fill in the letters of H*O*R*S*E

one at a time, making each shot
beyond the edges and top of the arc,
(the games of childhood go on till dark)

saving the free throw for last,
its cost immeasurable. It dances off the rim,
the sound still pinging in my chest.

The Family Name

Over the phone, each of us sounds out the same code,
a vain attempt to explain
the spelling of our name:
a slow S-A-L, then "C as in cat," M-A-N.
People get it wrong, hearing instead of the Czech C we pronounce
a German Z, not knowing
that was the first thing my father changed
at Ellis Island. Probably lost a T in there too
(his brother kept both) and an extra N at the end,
and anything else that would let you know
a pile of dust once pushed a cart of salt and spices
down a cobbled street.

The German lords in Slavic lands were free
to name their subjects for what they did:
tanner, smith, bishop, cook, and baker.
Centuries later you can pick their descendants out,
the Saxons who'd risen far enough to own a shop sign
or enter a guild and those forbidden to do either—

the Jews who sold meat, milk and roses in the snow or rain,
acquiring the honorific of "man,"
no longer just a "ben," a son of David or Jonah.

Confronted with the visual evidence of the C
our luck with the maître d', the editor,
the receptionist in the hotel lobby, is often no better—
they transcribe it into an O or E,
my family and I joined to the tribe
of those who sell or were sold, the children of Solomon.

INDECENT DESIRE

My heart still runs on phosphorous—
Diamond match heads eaten
behind a lumpy sofa chair in Brooklyn
and later, the guttered wax that fell to the floor
as I sawed at cardboard planks
and spilled candle flames at Passover
until my late uncle Ralph and father
half-feared a rubber tool kit and small mad Vulcan
would turn their Exodus to burnt-umber.
More to the point,
I once set an actual fire,
piling newsprint into an abandoned doorway
on East 7th Street
with a friend who outran my polio-
shriveled leg, leaving me there to watch
the crumpled polyhedrons burn
like shorn sea-urchins,
their spineless faces blackened with car wrecks and ads.
Thirty years later
the heart that runs on phosphorous
has stockpiled its fuel of discontent
awaiting a conflagration of desire
and a proper fuse.

CLEARING THE BRAMBLES

In Old Saybrook the braided trunks of cedars
shade my father's face, his legs askew
with the effort of carting lawn chairs to where we wait,
his gravitational platform deserting his desire
at ninety-five to play the host.

Drinks in our hands we drowse in the sun;
I watch him snatch at sleep like a cat,
gone and back in minutes, his neurons sputtering lamps
decades past the use-by date of his brain.

His nose twitches with the sun, its light flickers
in the maples and birches, rouses swarms of flies and gnats.
Later, my father and I put seed in the birder
but no cardinals come.

He gets up to work the brambles, pulling up branches
and straggling creepers, snapping them in two
on his knee. He's clearing this field for someone to sell to.

CUTTING APPLES

My father always carried a penknife
to pare his green apples, raising their skins
in perfect spirals. He never drew blood
slicing his bananas for breakfast,
their dark-seeded cores like little faces
dropping into the milk, one more item
in a life of a thousand chores,
one more notch in a life advancing
by millimeters or inches, not seconds or days.
I watched him turn himself as carefully away
from violence as a lathe on a table leg,
cutting each curve and flourish
from the flat face of a block
clamped in his hand. His hand and its thumb
never shied from the blade; no fool, he knew
what you do with any tool gives it value,
like a life—not too eager or afraid.

Three Deaths

I.
My mother's mother died of phlebitis
in a Bensonhurst apartment
that always smelled of face oil,
linoleum and paprika.
What remained of her life
before the war
were a tortoise shell comb,
a silver hair brush
and a gold cigarette lighter.

II.
Weeks after we buried Yanka,
her third husband jumped
from their sixth floor window.
None of us suspected such deep feeling
in Uncle Irwin, a man without appetite
who wouldn't spend a dime on his wife
alive and hated her smoking.

III.
The next year my mother died
giving a lecture at the library.
My father from his front row seat
could almost feel her fibrillating heart,
but the autopsy gave no clue
why she died so young.
He suspected grief was her assassin—
like some mysterious influenza.

I didn't cry—afraid that once I started,
I might set off a chain reaction
and kill someone else I loved. Even myself.

The Doctor Gets A Daughter

How fine your infant head was,
the still mobile sutures coming to rest
beneath my hand, meeting
in perfect serpentines, their edges
locked like continents.

You seemed as infinite as Jupiter then
but still I had to check: my unthinking finger
sought out your fontanel, dimpling
its soft red spot, the membrane pulsing
with possibility. It's good we forget

the first year the skull bone hardens, never know
the twilight when it softens again.
I suspect I treated you like a stranger.
It was early in the day when we met.

BITTERROOT

—for Menke Katz (1906-1991)

A hemophiliac in a razor blade factory,
a wisdom tooth in a small mouth.

They wanted to kill him right here,
far from Lithuania,

strip his great head of its attachments
and joy: unruly eyebrows, flatulent ears.

In his best poem he praised the potato
dark and silent in the ground.

He drew flowers on my every letter,
on rejection slips, on napkins.

He smelled of garlic, its bitter rose
and scallion root, useful

as foxglove's purple flower
or the silvered bud of belladonna.

Full of possibilities, he rode a headless horseman—
his head on his arm, his hat on his horse.

EVERYTHING BUT THE ASHES

If a man saves a single life
it's as if he saved the entire world—The Talmud

Saved by starvation Wiesenthal was too weak to kill himself.
The ninety-seven pounds that remained on his release
from Mauthausen couldn't stop his brain
from calculating ways to remember the others.
For the brain is a savage beast, it eats
when and what no other organ eats,
so the head and eyes become as large as a child's,
the body starves, extremities shrink
and the belly develops a paunch....
He said *I am the last...the one who can still speak,*
I will repeat and repeat and repeat this year's inventory:
bound for Berlin, twenty-five freight cars of women's hair,
248 of clothing, a hundred boxcars filled with shoes
and jewelry taken from the Jews;
400,000 watches, four thousand carats of diamonds,
one hundred and sixty tons of wedding rings—
the Germans shipped everything but their ashes.
He knew how a grand indictment like this might fit
on a lading slip, how a number might hold a memory.

After the war his brain was still hungry
so it went hunting. Ecce homo! In Sao Paolo,
Franz Stangl of Treblinka and Franz Wagner of Sobibor;
in Argentina, Josef Schwammberger of Poland;
in Vienna, Karl Silberbauer, the man who'd arrested Anne,
working as a policeman. Not counting Eichmann
that group was his biggest meal.
His brain snacked on frau Ryan, a housewife in Queens,
where the former queen of Maidenek lived without her whip,
and bit on a Romanian killer in Michigan who hid as an archbishop.
Not that he saw through every disguise:
he missed the Angel of Death.

All in all, he spent fifty years in Vienna,
a city that hated him like a poke in the eye,
surrounded by file cards and photos, affidavits and writs—
not a scrap was wasted. This was the life he had to give
and the metabolism of starvation its special gift.
When he died in his sleep at ninety-six
everything was shipped but the ashes.

Sea Nettles

—*Chrysaora quinquecirrha*

The trembling lampshade heads
and shivering arms
have no strange beauty to speak of—
no phosphor glows at night.
No bones, no heart, no brains, no eyes.
The day I no longer recall their name
I feel the onset of age
while hauling up
the anonymous curling slime
of tentacles on the anchor chain.
Whatever I once called them
there's no swimming in the midst of this,
so many small ones float by our boat
there's no safety reclining on a raft either,
the conditions precisely as they wish:
hot and humid, a briny mix.
If relief comes, hours later
it's not the name but the knowledge
of how forgetting goes:
life's awful and terrible things wiped first
some small resentments next,
before steering towards a final music,
the mind set free of memory.

Poem On A Single Word
From Richard Serra's Verb List

To cut: to sever, to divide, to incise,
to split from the herd,
to be snide, to make the body firm,
to heal the weak, to deride
a moon in front of its own sun,
to lay down a groove
and dance on a rug
with someone else's love.

To cut: to bleed, to render, to wound,
to shave a pitch
and make a fast ball rise, to dip
and leave a tackler miss,
to carve a block, to pass in front of,
to slice through a wave, to part
and cross, to gouge a ravine, to hew
or trim, to grow out teeth, to cleave.

Suppose You Miss The Lightning

"A poet is a man who manages…
to be struck by lightning five or six times."
—Randall Jarrell

It can happen—a lifetime of standing out
in thunderstorms, your head drenched
with good intentions, no one about
to save you—and nothing happens,

not a single hit, never mind the five or six
you need to qualify, much less the dozen
devoutly wished to signal greatness with,
a place in the universe of wordsmiths as fixed

as Regulus is in the heavens.
But the poet who made this famous quip
is much less read today and many have felt
his bitterness, returning free of a celestial singe

that might anoint them: if lightning glows in death
it does so faintly, struck off with the smell of prose.

The Urge To Jump

You will remember S —, how he spent his life afraid, mostly of his own impulse to throw himself off a bridge into the water or traffic below. He developed such fears long before he learned how common they were. How else would you explain the delayed leap Paul Celan made into the Seine, or Primo Levi's late tumble down a circular staircase? Their shadows were his shadow, reaching bright and slant; and he knew that shadow had the power to kill. With the passing years, new problems developed: S — came to fear holding a baby lest he wring its neck or bang its head; he agonized over potentially impairing his patients by cutting their spinal cords and brains with a slip of his scalpel; he began to weigh the ease of turning such a whim into fate, to imagine each disaster an unhappy accident. In his meditations, S — recalled a story by Poe, "The Imp of the Perverse," in which the narrator struggles with fear of himself. This felt right to him — fear alone could make you do dreadful things. We can hardly blame S — for wanting to remain in his room until the temptation to do something awful had passed. Only then might he be capable of going out into the street, like any normal man, to walk among us. More and more S — stayed in his room and wrote, cocooned in his fear. In this private space, surrounded by books, his hours grew into days and months. Before he knew it a year had passed and then another wasted away and soon enough he was out of money and no one would bring him his food anymore. He starved and still he couldn't leave the apartment fearing that he might do the unthinkable. After all, how would he know when it was safe to come out? That awful urge to jump might grab him anywhere. But not there, not in his room, where they found him, his bed covered with pages, as Cocteau said of Proust — one felt the scattered papers still ticked, like the watches on the wrists of dead soldiers.

THE BODY PAINTED IN GRIEF

The sick man knows a single landscape,
a single artist, a single sun.
In the good spring two rocks
on the horizon shimmer from winter melt
flowing through them like kidneys relieving
the body of waste. And the hills beyond
are lungs, their gray mist and purple
flowers a deep breath from the rain.
The coiled valley below
crawls with colon-shaped bugs
transforming
succulence into nightshade.
Everywhere the pulse of crickets
as if this weekend life's sound were too busy to stop.
And though he can't see the high chapel above
the snow-white sheets,
he can hear the words
the body is softly preaching: pain is the sign
the brain must believe in and nothing but.

METONYMY: PART FOR THE WHOLE

Often unable to say or spell
what was there from the start,
it's easier to think Big Bang
while all creation drifts apart

at increasing speed: cows
and men, stars, houses, all of us flying
every which way from the center
throwing over the certainty of rows
and columns, displacing God
just as the red shift predicts.

Then why this persistent sense
that my small hand stands for all of me
and I'm one with the universe,
its birth and death, its blessing, its curse?

ELEGY: SAUL BELLOW

A tummler, a peddler, a pool shark, a prince,
a spinner of sentences;
explicator of the truth in lies
and the lies in truth,
a philosopher in a fancy suit
and tie, a rabbi in a fedora,
a wandering Jew.
Just think of the deep pronouncement
his name makes—bellow—
he could shout about Chicago genes
but was really a polyglot of nations
and cities like Kiev and Montreal.
He could crow on The Loop or cry in Boston,
laugh about his presumption
that a shrimp like him
was catnip to the girls.
Elegant but unfashionable, smart
but not clever, a runt but not a mutt,
a son of The Book and its two types of flame,
burning black letters and sizzling white page.

Turner Sets Out In A Snowstorm

JMW Turner, in his last decade
wishing to paint a steamboat in a snow storm,
had himself strapped
to the *Ariel's* swinging mast for four hours.
Only five foot three
he held to his perch with bitter rope and stood
like a great unblinking owl
dreaming of a locomotive throwing off steam
while smoke and spray billowed and foamed
across the decks and almost swept him clear.
All the while, his frozen gaze tongued the napes
of boarding waves like maidens' necks, while bits
of salt clotted the sheets and his rime-hung
lashes. When the white caps at last whipped off
the wave tops, wind frothed the air he breathed
and the lung of the storm gagged him;
it turned the ocean to steam and stung his brow
with ice drops shaped like diamonds.
So much pain he endured to paint a souvenir
of the real: a ship slides down
a red and yellow maelstrom and hurtles itself at us,
at him, as an engine does on watery tracks.

THE ROUGH AND THE SMOOTH
—The Four Backs, 1909-1931

The first time Matisse made one
her back emerged from a bronze plaque
against the wall
like the Rockies pushing up
the Continental Divide; in his second try
she's cracked jewels and crags
of dolomite and limestone. God with Adam
he goes back to the clay
and smooths her down, the background
erupting like tectonic plates covering
her over, her thick braid of hair
hanging down like that plumb line
he used in school and kept to
ever after, apprenticed to Buonarotti's slaves
disgorged in their blocks, and Rodin's hands
held straight as God's in heaven…

He kept it in his pocket,
a small teardrop of lead and a bit of twine,
and took it out now.
Smoother and smoother she became;
the last bas relief almost recedes into the wall
and the trigonometry of her spine
takes over, the straight line seeking
the earth's center, plumbing its depths
like the lead we trail behind
our little ship of state:
the dreaming brain, crossing its ocean.

THE DOG SPEAKS

—Interior With Dog by Matisse, 1934

I'm only half-asleep so I know you're standing there
wondering if I'm asleep. Nope.
It's not easy to rest under this table—
for one thing, there's a strong downward slope
and gravity's got me half tipped out of my basket
like an apple by Cezanne.
Talk about a flat world!
For another, I can't get away from these colors,
the red floor tiles, orange table leg
and pink wall burning on my lids like the sun.
Then again I'm never alone; the kids think a gray dog is cute
and I'm the only dog in the room. I was bribed
(that's my excuse) with a bone
and a bowl of fresh water. Really,
I wish you wouldn't stare—it's extra hard to be an icon
when you're not an odalisque and have no hair.
Here's the inside dope, he wore a vest when he painted *them*
but saved his housecoat for *me*. I liked sitting for him,
he was never rude and spared me his violin.
I think I look very dignified, not naked, just nude.

In The Lost Movie Of Its Making, Pollock's Red Canvas

—for Kirk Varnedoe (1946-2003)

In the lost movie of its making
the flat bed of metaphor fell:

blood red, heart red, the wine dark sea.
In the first frame you threw a coagulum of paint

its black skeins a tracery of neurons
igniting each movement of your arm,

the dance of your feet; you thinking jazz,
me thinking Yeats. In the second frame lost

dabs of aluminum spilled from liberty boats built
at the Navy Yard in Brooklyn

or that silver nosed bomb hung over
a Japanese sea. In the third frame we spy

a fugitive word, "Jackson" or "Lee,"
even your boast, "Hans, I *am* nature"

written in your seminal code,
the white nucleic twists crossing in red and black arcs.

In the movie's last frame the back end of your brush
flings midnight at an arabesque of cracks,

the memory perhaps of your father as he pees
atop Indian rocks, showing his boy how it gets done

and you so lost in the film of finding your painting
pour on its meaning before stitching it up.

An Uncommitted Crime

—Art is an uncommitted crime (Adorno)

Oscar Wilde must have thought so
before he read Cellini's autobiography
in which, the maker of that gold and enamel saltcellar
said he crucified a man just to see more accurately
how his tendons moved and muscles twitched.
Pope Clement naturally forgave him,
since art was the real point of suffering
and not the redemption of sin.

Contra Chekhov

The gun never went off: not in the first act, not in the second, not even in the third. Of course, it was meant to be a rifle hanging on a wall and not a pistol, certainly not a popgun. But there it was, a weapon so small and portable, it was not easily noticed by the audience, something you could hide away in a table with a single drawer and a top of in-laid green parchment, a color dark enough not to clash with the old prints hanging on the hallway wall. Therefore, the fact that it never went off created hardly any disappointment, not in the general public and not in the near relatives and other witnesses in the audience surrounded by images of much bigger, noisier guns fired off by their owners on every conceivable occasion, not just in drawing rooms but in church, in the halls of government, in the streets of modest suburbs. The absence of noise might have been more disturbing than the absence of action if not for the surfeit of noise and action in every book, television show and film, not to mention the theater of life, with its electronic devices and absence of silence. Making a silence was now the equivalent of making a noise and the owner of the not-quite-big-enough gun considered inaction a kind of protest, an almost invisible movement against the roaring tide.

At Green River Cemetery

Grieving for Lady Day,
Frank O'Hara would have called the neighbors "fancy fags"
too, like my friend Will does, looking at
their Mark Hampton antiques,
a mahogany and brass runabout from the '40s
ornamenting the grass,
some topiary and purple flowers on the trellis.

In the Hamptons the "trade parade" begins at three,
the Ford pick-ups, Suburu sedans, SUVs
in caravan to Middle Island
where off-the-res Shinnecocks and Montauketts live
when not servicing plutocrats north and south
of "the avenue." Some other workers are descendants
of black slaves and white whalers who built up Sag
and wound up driven back by the dunes and clumps of sea grass
where Walt once walked and Melville wrote
of Queequeg's misery
visiting the rich fisher folk who worshipped money,
their industry notwithstanding.

Out at Green River Cemetery,
where there's no river by any name,
all the artists have monuments but O'Hara—
his flat tile stuck in the ground, his grave over-run by shadows.

A flowering beech stands guard in the wind
and somewhere behind the big estates and high hedges
thick as stone was the Sound we couldn't hear.

Baltimore Was Always Blue

Goodbye America of the blue overalls and steel-toed boots,
goodbye, goodbye. The headline in *The Sun* said it all today
in type as tall as the election of a president:
General Motors Closes Its Broening Highway Plant.
Don't you remember when they said what was good for GM
was good for America? In the Forties they called men like Bob
at the gym "expediters"—they sorted parts for fifty cents
an hour, everything in its proper place at the right time.
Goodbye to you and the smell of cayenne and cinnamon
drifting over the Inner Harbor when it had rotting piers
and McCormick Spice. Goodbye, goodbye General Mills,
Bendix and Western Electric, farewell to the steel plate
and memories of Liberty ships, their hulls bent true and shaped
at Sparrows Point by thirty thousand hands. Goodbye
to London Fog, its raincoats and umbrellas, "Born in Baltimore,
Raised Everywhere," and sterling silver candlesticks
turned on lathes in Hamden. Goodbye steel beams,
locomotives and trains, automobiles and ships,
military bombers, telephones, stoves and Natty Bo Beer.
Over half a century, a city dies a thousand cuts: condos rise
where breweries stood, the Ritz-Carlton goes up at Beth Steel,
and office towers are put where Proctor and Gamble made soap
on the harbor. Near Seagirt Marine, 7000 men (and women too)
made metal vans, things on wheels we import from Japan.
For seventy years, while New York and Chicago wore tweed
topcoats and gray fedoras, Baltimore was dressed in blue.
Now it's goodbye to factory whistles, tin hats, lunch pails
filled with ham and mayonnaise. No welders eat Italian
on Holabird Avenue, no salesmen sleep
at the Brentwood and Carson Inns, no one raises a shot to a crab
at the Poncabird Pub. It's goodbye to all that.

THE LONG-AGO DEAD

In Aufderheide's big book of mummies
the long-ago dead look and don't look a lot like us.
The omnivorous eye survives best,
in ninety-three percent of those with heads,
the water inside draining so fast
its shriveled orb and optic nerve resemble
a wild chanterelle or a walnut wild with seeing.
And next most often is hair,
whether dried in a desert cave or frozen by ice,
preserved with a note of fashion
or a family's last loving kindness, lush tresses
combed and braided, or flat and in plaits.
You may imagine such a text is not too shy about sex:
penises persist beyond all sense and sensation,
even as they do in life. Not the breasts, however.
Of the brain and the rest there's little more to say—
almost nothing survives but fine powder
and a little bone it wears like a cap.

CAESAR'S LAST BREATH

On the Ides of March, great Caesar stabbed to death
by friends, expelled his final breath
in exclamation, an accusation I'm forced to share
by Fermi's calculation each time I respire in joy or despair
inhaling the cry my mother gave in giving me birth
or later, my father's shout at exchanging the earth
beneath our feet, from blooded Old World to New.

What holds the star-winged atoms of our bones but the glue
of universal speech, the pneuma of life:
each day exchanges the oxygen of kings with child and wife,
the lips of long gone fiends exclaim with those in doubt
of divinity or pray in unison with the most devout.

Less a calculus of breath than perverted fate,
how often we exhale our loves and fill our lungs with hate.

THE APPRENTICE SURGEON

Death is the mother of beauty—Wallace Stevens

How awful for him to cut the flesh or watch
a deep cut made before carbolic acid,
before ether, before hope was more than a wretch
on the kerb of the roadside, lungs etched

with cavitation and fawn-colored phlegm.
He knew how death would cork his mouth, killing his speech,
its beauty and necessity. Keats was an apprentice then
to death, his own and all of life beyond its reach:

the nightingale song, the clay of ancient Greece,
and that season of reconciliation for which he longed.
Entombed in life he felt no peace,
despaired of fame and got much else wrong

while setting some right: dreamed of autumnal skies
standing at the bedside, attending to the horror at Guy's.

INTENSIVE CARE

I am called at 3 in the morning
to examine the dead:
nightclothes puddled around
a face the color of cocoa,
cornrows and braids
stiff on the unseeing head,
surrounded by her extended family.
I watch
her heart squeeze
blood into her brain
until stunned
clear water flows
like tears down a long tube
and drains in a plastic bag.
At five o'clock I pronounce
some of her dead—
the pupils that fail to see,
the ears that no longer hear,
even the limbs that fail to move
with all the pain I can give.
But her killer heart lights up
orange and red,
winks and whistles at me,
beating a tattoo of victory.

MOTHER OF THE BAY

We sit in the bottle-necked mouth of the Corsica,
my boat and I, four hundred miles south
of the river's birth, stirring a fugitive part of the Bay
where the current slows down and the bottom lifts
its shallow fist in a wave, daring my keel
to pass over. But my head still throbs

from last night's wine and worse, the noise of geese
rising in the fields to distract me.
Entering the cut, I'm in and out in a moment,
overtaken with a flood rising like memory,
where the estuary seems immortal and choked with life.
Too rushed to despair, I steer and pass by.

Not too many think of her now
in the old Indian way—say Susquehanna slowly
and what you hear is Mother of the Bay;
she comes with poison today
gathered from coalfields, blooming algae
in silt and debris, trapping oyster and crab

in nitrate and shale, drowning life in life.
The Susquehanna flows past ravaged hills, skips
and swashes on broad-faced stones long-settled
in the Flats, drives quickly past a million oaks,
their stances cocked on cliffs, their branches burning
as she rolls from Wilmington and North East

to Rising Sun and Aberdeen, all those towns between
Baltimore and Philadelphia, stitched like cowry shells
in the terrain of an inland sea
glaciers gouged eons before shellfish calmed
its underwater garden. In Elk's Neck, Elkton,
and Newark, and throughout the Bush River,

the snowmelt drains from far in the throats
of Adirondack creeks, adding fresh water to the mix
of ocean brack and grasses making up the Chesapeake:
a Susquehannock word for *great river*
where strange fish with hard coverings lay—unknowing
in giving a name to our Bay, praying for its survival.

A SEASON LIKE THIS

The news was full of death
and the green plants grew
big beyond their means
fed by the incessant rain.
No hyacinths bloomed
in our back yard,
no fire proof stems.
Perhaps you are too young to remember
a season like this
where even our pets
fell out of sorts
and people were irritable.
Neighbors gathered on corners
to brawl after turning off
their TV sets.
Sometimes a punch
was thrown
or a hand
would lift up a stone
and test its sharp edges.
No one could tell when summer came
or if they were heading for fall.
It went on like this for a year;
no one could read the weather
and most didn't want to.

Bird On A Wire

His small feet sit like calipers
judging the distance to the junction box
his eye on an old glass terminal;
his beak doesn't spark with electricity
this first day two feet of snow have melted
enough there's more green than white
outside my window.
                The sparrow seems
not as cold as the ground, not as frozen
as the sky, but still very still
as if thinking it out, how unconquerable
he is, a gray protein sac against a gray sky
waiting it out.

I Gave My Ticket To A Blind Man
At Oriole Park

He stood alone at the turnstile, tall and pear-shaped
like Louis-Philippe, and held a cane
bare of bronze or gold;
he seemed to hold it tightly close like a raptor's beak,
while he waited for me.

He might have stayed at home,
ear pressed to the radio, listening to the play by play,
but thirteen times he's come to the ballpark,
just this season,
to see the game in the sunshiny dark—

he can feel the rush of the crowd as they rise to cheer,
he can taste the weather on his face,
the breeze on his lashes, the June warmth in his ear,
even the shadows slanting as they race across the outfield.

I lead him to the bleachers
and try to imagine his anticipation—
in the midst of thirty thousand sighted strangers,
I feel it growing on my tongue
as I wait to be seen by you.

LAST SATURDAY MORNING IN BOULDER

—for Bob Cooperman

Who but you remembers one-armed Earl,
who played guitar with a match book cover
folded in his metal claw, while I sang
in Roxbury flats, smoke-filled before the riots,
or that I came back to Brooklyn
when your father died thirty years ago?
It's a long time for two friends to lose their hold
of one another before reconnecting at the foot
of the continental divide
not too far from a book shop
selling everlasting enlightenment
and goddess apparel, on Pearl Street with our wives.

Mountains of fresh air have not cured
your tongue of its foul and ranting accompaniment—
it scalds me erupting from your circumoral beard;
you look more and more like Jerry Garcia
or a Colorado miner, your eyes as big
as pans sifting for gold.
                              What else do I remember
from that Saturday morning in Boulder?
That you still thrum your fist
on the table, that you still pinch your nose to drive
your glasses back up its slope—
my mind making these notes
without daring to look at your hand, its scarred wrist
and tangled mound of tendons hid
by a generous nature. Only later, I remember
how you ran laughing into that plate glass door,
shattered after a raucous game of stickball
in the street, and we stopped keeping score—
since only one could still become a surgeon
and I knew who the real writer would be.

A Song Of Spirals

I stand at the water's edge with you
and lift my eyes to stare
at a small corner of creation, a milky smear

in which dim stars whirl
and a bright nebula sits at the foot of Orion.
I have no telescope to see them by

so memory resurrects the pattern
of newborn stars rushing in a pinwheel
like Shiva's arms, the cosmos whorled as tight

as my thumb. We seek its pattern everywhere,
from star clusters to pine cones
to petals on a stem,

until our inner ear and the snail in its shell
seem rigged together in a plan you might call divine
(or others intelligent design?),

one that plausibly began with rabbits—

Leonardo Pisano shared their leporine wish to multiply.
In 1202, he wanted to know how many pairs would ensue
if he walled-up two hares in a garden

and abolished death. He discovered a series of digits
converging to a golden mean
by which Fibonacci, as he called himself,

reshaped the world as less random than before.
It must have seemed a miracle then—
it still does now,

as if God had moved to Pisa and changed His name to Pisano.
Tonight his song of spirals plays in my ear,
in a galaxy of cells hooked like a sea horse,

a deep B-flat rings in the gyred organ of my brain
and memorializes me. Without a thought, I press my flesh
to the mouth of a Nautilus and holding its shell

feel hopelessly redundant—

who else would cradle this almost ceramic skin
and listen to the ocean in remove
while standing at its edge?

I know the memory of its rush will slip away, all of us
born with an entropy the stars have never known.
Unpredicted and unique, how do we share

our stave of skin, our music of disposition?
I bend to kiss your ear, cheered by its imperfection,
its baby pink shell a broken spiral of cartilage,

and think intelligent design nothing, nothing but a guess.

HEAT LIGHTNING

Tonight's appointment with Mars is canceled,
it hangs invisible, its orange light shuttered
by incessant mist. There's nothing much to see
but heat lightning candling the clouds for monsters.
Forced to sit at anchor, we watch the crabbers haul up
their catch on Trippe Creek or pause to unravel
at dawn what the dampness grows, spiders re-spinning
their webs binnacle to boom, boom to wheel.

Sixty thousand years have passed since Mars approached
this near and someone else, perhaps more innocent,
also wondered what to call an unknown light hanging
above the trees, its surprise as sweet as berries
on the tongue. Not the word for war or god or chief,
not the name he calls himself or members of his clan;
not Mars. Did his word inhabit a sound we humans use today
or was it only a thought without the gift of speech?

Three days in, the weather lifts, and turning southeast,
a planet rises, its rounded silence forms on my lips;
"Oh", I think, he must have paused his breath like this.

Zamboni

Charlie Brown once said
there are three things in life that people like
to stare at: a flowing stream, a crackling fire
and a Zamboni machine clearing the ice.

Made nowhere near where water naturally freezes,
the Zamboni factory sits in the side street sprawl
of south Los Angeles, between Compton
and Bellflower, where industry and strip malls meet.

Made square like a gunnery box from World War Two,
they test a new Zamboni on a block of Colorado Avenue
where it trudges to the corner KFC at a speed
of nine miles per hour, then stops and whirls about

to be checked for leaks; if the Zamboni passes
it's fitted with studded tires and a handwritten tag on a string
telling where to ship it:
Prague or Dubai or an ice rink in Milwaukee.

The Zamboni moves in slow ovals, like a cow,
scraping the ruts and gathering the shavings in a metal box
using hidden augers in its guts.
Then whizzes some water out and gives the ice a sheen.

The children in their ski hats cheer
each time the Zamboni takes the ice
in between periods of the game and boo
if some patch has been left less than perfect.

Men scraped and shoveled and sprayed the ice until 1949
when this rough beast appeared with its lovely name—
Zamboni. The company asks you not to use it as an adjective or noun
but I love its sound and that my Mother's favorite skater

Sonja Henie bought the first two.

THE ENEMY OF GOOD IS BETTER

You've gone back and forth dozens of times
trying to make her understand
but it only gets worse.
The air is blue with words.
In her mind it's enough to say *I'm sorry* that first time.

But you persist to sharpen the argument
as if peeling the skin off a grape—
(it will bruise before it bursts)
or doing an aneurysm in a valley of the patient's brain,
your operating hand more eager to grab
its neck in a clip than your own brain
thinking you'll sharpen its edges just a bit,
make everything as straight as an autopsy
and it will all be better.

But enough was enough before it got angry
and a bright burst of blood fills the valley
with regret. You wish you had stopped sooner,
what was good enough to cure is gone
and what is better has left you a ruin

WATER PSALM FOR ST. MICHAEL'S

Late spring on the Chesapeake,
early summer. The boats scud
to a stop in St. Michael's harbor,
their white wings folded like water birds
their necks bent
to the earth by anchor chains.
In this place I hear nothing against
the silence of my nature,
nothing man-made or shrill.
Here are sailors below and there,
a stepped horizon made
of church spires
and a screw-pile lighthouse,
its amber light beyond the power
of its own machinery, like Delft's—
a calm beyond Vermeer.
Not all that passes through my eye's
pupil is ever impaled
on a page of chemical light. Today
the least snap aspires
to the condition of art
and art to the condition of music;
but truth's a prayer we offer up
to a clouded sky, our sight
and seeing made in a halo of droplets.
Put your camera down, I say
no picture can smell this sweet.

NAVIGATION

If this, then that
a sharp edge, a cut.

The spring you came back
fireflies danced

over the graves of cicadas
and the engine died

in a narrow waterway:
among sloops at anchor

and an audience of mariners,
their coolers and pets,

watched my discomfort.
And what you may care

about such perilous navigation,
my making way barely

without a breath, my hand
turning the wheel

so slowly, I can't imagine.

Scenes From A Marriage:

1- Al Fresco

In my reverie,
the cool Tuscan air slides down my neck
your damp brow and bare breast
moist with early summer, wet
with expectation. You breathe slowly
above a white scoop of roses
stitched blue and red onto your dress
and a thin band of Florentine gold
around your neck,
bought on the Ponte Vecchio
twenty summers ago, when our daughter
hung like a great melon between your hips
and I stood alone at the Arno.
Too poor to buy you earrings then,
then out of love with you, and after—me,
when it didn't seem we'd ever see
these narrow streets together,
nor I this bodega again.

Now standing outside the door with you,
on a day cooler than I remember,
the weather slowly changes in its airy ocean
like the heart does—
unknowing in its motion—
and your neck is bare.
When we hear the bell in the bodega ring,
you don't take my hand.
Perhaps you've lost it—
the necklace I mean,

it hasn't circled your throat in years,
not home, not here, not now
as the shop door closes and you rush
across the bridge in a bright blue pantsuit,
not stopping once for sentiment,
not searching in my shop of wonders
where just twenty summers ago
a goldsmith wished me a life of luck.

2- Route 101 Heading South

On the drive from Gleneden to Florence,
clusters of yellow grapes on the hillsides
flash bright as the median stripe on the highway.

At Moolack Beach, an odor sweeps
across the road—blood beneath
the fish flesh, guano and seaweed,

also salmonberry, thimbleberry, wild current and gorse
wildflowers whose perfume
makes me raise the electric window

so I won't fly out over the ocean,
a cormorant circling on ax-head wings,
set free from the fog-bound shore.

3- Drowsy

In the dizzy warmth after sex,
your head rests on the pillow
of my arm, a xylophone

of bone, I flex, feel press, let
go, as our two breaths
harmonic row towards sleep,
that sly thief of life
and meaning; it clothes us
in dreams and one another, wraps
us in the cerements of grief,
and steals away the hours.

4- Kiss The Coffin

Love never occupies the same moment
of time for any two people; one falls
first, the other swims behind
and, at the end, one walks away
and the other wonders why.
If it lasts, they die, separately.
You know what I'm saying—
I can see you yelling with your eyes.

5- This Spring in Baltimore

Eight miles in the city air
is heavy with the Bay
its salt smell lofts over
civilian oaks, crisps
the morning, alerts my face.
I ask a friend if she smells the piers
and moorings in my back yard,
the tide that laps the pyracantha?
It's not a dream, I say.
Just hours ago, its aroma hung

like stars in the treetops—
their grounded masts resplendent
their branches broken spars.

6- Unruly Nouns

They call it congress, union
as if we'd voted to be here, upside down
two crabs floating in the sheets
as if we could ever be united,
two different sparks of light
molted from the sun's bright ovum.

They call it intercourse, hunger fed
as if we were a pair of highways
meeting in a Persian knot
or two minds meeting in a room
full of solitaries,
as if two bodies fucking
could sweat out so many
hydrocarbons
without the sustenance of real food.

They call it lust—
as if we couldn't tell the difference.

7- Still Pond On The Bay

In Still Pond's cove I swam in water
thick with algae and the soup of life.

At night we lay on the hatches speaking
of you, the black sky rimmed with green,
watching a slow tide move out past the inlet
and other boats at anchor—
their mast-top lights like Christmas
ornaments, a child had tacked to the sky.

Amid the desolation felt by the first sailors
to these shores,
comfort seems a discovery.

Your image came to me
with the low sound of distant oceans
and vanished
when a rockfish jumped, its ringlets breaking
the rippled spine of the moon.

8- Rehearsing The End

Tonight she's still a baroness
her eyes hydrangeas,
drowned flowers, lacustrine,
her celadon dress
wrapped around a water-filled heart.

It's impossible to make
a finish—there's no feeling left
but you still meet, trees
touching sky at twilight,
your fingers, your knees,
on occasion your lips, brisk
to the point of hypothesis:
if only I could revise

the relationship like a poem,
rewrite it a thousand times,
perhaps it would shorten into
itself, be perfect, be gone.

But my shoulders hunch, the wish
for a martini, extra dry
is adamantine. I've read my Ruskin—
she's as bright as Venice
in her efflorescence of decay,
still shining. Don't let your eyes
slide from the sky to the lagoon.
Go ahead,
have another drink. It's time.

PUTTING THE BOAT IN

It's just sailing to you, but not to me,
my head afloat in fog and sun,
still charmed by its schoolboy physics:
at all angles but one a sailboat's not pushed
by wind but sucked forward—
its keel, mast and sail a single wing
weaving two oceans into one.

In Aprils past our boat went in
its wraps stripped off, its bright work done
but rebuilding the diesel wasted a month
and the rain didn't help us to hurry
this year despite good reason:
a need to incline our bodies one
against one, pale heliotropes in the sun.

But at last we're in, it's early May
and looking down I see a gray sky move
like a river laced with clouds of gin,
my face springing with clear runnels.
One of us cries or laughs, diverting my gaze—
I hide my water-stained head and bend
to the coaming, timing the passing wave.

THE PAINTED NIGHTGOWN

—after a painting by Julie Roberts

The night was red—
billowing behind her night dress
which flew disembodied over the ground
shoulders and waist ballooned out
by pure spirit
by an absence of flesh that made it jump
on pillows and turn around in the mirror
with joy, its gray cotton tick streaked
with autumn colors running
together like leaves dammed up
at the mouth of a river
its flannel voice still
its shadow hovering like the bell
of an ancient ear trumpet
listening to the night.

To The Mistress Of The Master
Of The Female Half-Lengths

— Flemish (c.1520-1540)

At the day sale, you were not quite fit for the bins
so you settled into an auction of the Circle of,
in the Manner of, from the School of and other has-beens
in the house of Art, where your delicate porcelain face
arched brows and hair parted in the middle,
might better startle the casual reader of the catalog
looking upon your slender manicured fingers and,
balanced above, an oval head and bare shoulders
turned three-quarters at your writing desk.

One hand lifts a book page, the other rests near a metal pot
of salve, the emblem of the Magdalene,
and through the window a balustrade and beyond that
a blue and green smoky landscape lifted from Leonardo.
What does it mean if your painter is known today only
as a Follower of the Master of the Female Half-Lengths,
an unknown epigone or sly copyist of some other artist
barely better limned than you, a man without a proper name
or history, rescued from the Flemish dark at the start
of a more modern era?

In this sale of authentic unknowns, among the sad pieties
of forgotten old masters who never were more inspired
than a carpenter plumbing a joist for a door,
his picture of you carries the meanest price;
it seems at least two men painted you over and over
as if sawing in half the same woman in their minds,
and their bootless fame, free of any personal gain
has lit your face with the grace of anonymity.

FROM
A PRAGUE SPRING, BEFORE & AFTER
(2016)

When you knock on the door of strangers,
there are three possibilities: they will send you away,
they will take you in, they will report you

PROLOGUE

Ladies and gentlemen, and children of all ages,
I welcome you to Prague, the capital of Bohemia,
of Czechoslovakia, of the Czech Republic,
and all too briefly the Holy Roman Empire
and the seat of the goddess of history.
Welcome to the Prague of Apollinaire
and his Jewish guide, Haman's king Ahasuerus,
to the Prague of Arcimboldo's carrot noses
and squash ears, mislabeled a poet by Bolaño
in 2666 and not a painter of portraits in corncobs
and peas, of Rudolf II and his *wunderkammer*,
of the equally wonderful rag picker's stalls
in the Jewish ghetto before Joseph cleared the slums,
of the Charles Bridge built with mortarized egg yolk
and egg shells, the Magic Prague of Ripellino,
and the New Jerusalem of the Jews
and the Museum to a Vanished Race
built in a synagogue by Germans.

This is the Prague of Hussites and Catholics
and the twice-hated Jews, German-speaking like Kafka,
of the dead who do not speak
and of the dead who do.

Welcome to the mausoleum of misnamed streets
and embankments, of embalmed astrophysical ghosts
like Tycho Brahe and Kepler, of Freud and Mahler
on their country walks, of Einstein and Rilke
speaking in tongues, even in the same room.

Welcome to the pandemonium and sorrow
where next to time language is the slippery eel
of history, where every tongue slides back
into the Moldau and the river's weirs,
where all will be swallowed up by the jaws
of a city strung like a whistling harp.

1944

1. (The Dead)

These dead have no faces: Father's five brothers-in-law,
all but one sister, his own father and mother,
my mother's father, my little cousins.

God knows why a family as large as a town
was erased; smoke and fire belched
from Moloch's mouth and the earth shook.

After they were gone, I never looked again
at the old brown photographs, nameless and worthless
like the deeds to blown-up houses,

without my Father forcing me to,
me forgetting the first while he still spoke
of the last. How dark a sun will set with him.

When you knock on the door of strangers,
there are three possibilities: they will send you away,
they will take you in, they will report you.

2. (Meeting Miklos Szabo)

My Father and I sit on the train to Ardley-on-Hudson.
It's the first time I meet Miklos Szabo,
Czech partisan, good Catholic, polite anti-Semite,

the doppelgänger he wore like a cloak in 1944;
memory flashes in Father's brain
like the summer river sparkling below.

In sixty years, it's the first time I've heard the name
of his partner in escape, how they fought against
the Germans and ran from home-grown Nazis.

Did one or both jump from a window,
live in a cellar, put a strong arm to a widow?
Perhaps he named me Michael in honor of

his alter ego or because we share the same
narrow lips and nose, the same cold eye.

3. (The Factory)

From Poša to Liptovský, the SS pursued him west,
where a friend sent him to run a tractor factory.
One day, a German soldier asked,

"Aren't you the Jew S—, Arthur?"
and my Father stuck his nose into his face and said,
"I'm Szabo, Miklos, a good Catholic and who are you

to call me anything; you're probably a goddamn Jew,
not me!" After the officer left, my Father knew
his time in Liptovksý was up; so he fled further west

to Banská Bystrica and joined the partisans there,
some of whom hated a Jew more than a German.
Captured by the Germans on Mt. Kyslinky,

his band was jailed in a schoolhouse for three days,
not time enough to get a number or a seat on a train.

4. (Defenestration)

Even three days was too much for the men
of the Resistance after ten thousand had died
and the town of Lidice was burnt alive and flattened

in revenge for the assassination of Heydrich,
the Hangman of Prague. That my Father jumped
from the first floor window of that schoolhouse

and survived was in the best Czech tradition,
the Thirty Years War having started in 1618
when two Catholic governors were thrown from the Hrad

and saved by a pile of dung, and the Hussite rebellion
two centuries before in which city councilors were chucked
from the New Town Hall and finished off with pikes.

The station master was a partisan, and that's where Father ran
to hide—he needed time to flee further west.

5. (In The Cellar)

He told the woman who hid him next
beneath scraps of scavenged copper
that the partisans would blow up her home

if she didn't help. When the cellar opened
he found the Laufers, husband and wife
and their nine year old girl shitting

in a pail, eating a crust of bread
the landlady hung from a cord
so she wouldn't have to touch a Jew.

Even in jail they cut them out,
where Slovaks and Czechs parted like waves
from their circumcised brethren.

Life in the cellar must have been
like being trapped in a submarine
or caught in a collapsed coal mine,

your fear of dogs and Germans and death
descending on your head
as the earth was pitched on your grave.

For three weeks, terror pricked like Noah's rain;
my Father changed his name and uniform once a day.

6. (The Truck)

From where they were hiding, my Father said
you could see the truck ride out in the morning,
men and shovels packed in its bed, the guards

having a smoke, the men shouldering their rakes and tools
as if going to work, as if volunteering.
It was a small town; people out walking could see them go.

In the afternoon, from where you were hiding
you could hear the shots, then nothing
until the truck returned, its belly rumbling back

for another meal, the guards having a smoke,
the tools laid down neatly in a stack
where the men once stood;

even from hiding, you could see people on the street
give the driver a wave, his tarp filthy with dirt.

7. (Arnold)

The three of them stood on the platform
at a switching point: my cousin Arnold, his father
and Death, waiting for the train to Terezín.

Arnold was thirteen but jumped into a freight car
going the wrong way, giving his father's hand
a final squeeze before making his move.

Even though they were losing, running out of gas
and gunshot shells, the Germans felt
they had time enough to finish their project.

On the last great march out of Terezín,
they shot the prisoners who couldn't keep up;
even his guard begged Arnold's father not to stop walking

or else he would be forced to shoot him. I wonder
where he put the bullet, in what part of the skull.

8. (Magda)

Three times my cousin Magda stood naked in the snow,
selected by Mengele himself, the Angel of Death;
three times she wisely declined the kindness of his gift

switching lines to be with older and healthier girls.
Once he asked her "Aren't you only thirteen?"
but Magda said "No, your ledger's wrong, I'm sixteen and fit

for work." He slapped her gently on the cheek
and motioned her the other way, like God writing
in the Book of Life on the Day of Atonement.

She often stamped her feet and slapped her face
to bring her color up, sometimes bit the inside of her cheek
but her blood had dried up from thirst.

Today she's still beautiful, colored like my Mother in late bloom
and nervous as a cat; but not everything in her has survived.

9. (The Pinkas Synagogue)

When you knock on the door of strangers,
there are three possibilities: they will send you away,
they will take you in, they will report you.

I didn't know where to find their names,
the farmer and his wife, the two daughters,
the righteous gentiles my cousin Arnold had them inscribe

on the walls of the Pinkas Synagogue,
close by the names of those they couldn't save.
Then a flood came and wiped the walls clean

for a bit as if God too wished to erase them.
Outside this wall and the old Jewish cemetery,
the Czechs have built a Museum of Decorative Arts,

the stacked stones and red letters like shards
of Bohemian glass, cutting the soul. Like knives.

10. (Alfred)

What would we do without the records the killers kept
when there's no one left with blue green numbers?
I never thought to ask my cousin Magda, Uncle Alfred

or my stepmother Lilly if they spoke or met
in the place with a name like God's
too terrible to speak; it would shame me to remember—

my Father knows this. After the war, he found his brother
in a hospital, a stick leaning on a stick,
an insect on a branch; the man didn't know his brother's face.

This was the end of his war-time romance:
Father paused and never said if running his race to freedom
was better than the camps,

never explained why the world has no pity for the living
or why a boy like me loved trains but hated tracks.

QUESTIONS FOR KAFKA

Is it better not to know why they want to kill you?
Is it better to wear an initial or a number?
Is it better to be abandoned by God or to abandon Him?
Is it good to speak the language of your oppressor?
If you knew what they called your people in their holy book,
what would you have chosen, to be a rat or a flea?
In retrospect, is the cockroach not too noble?
Is it better to change or not survive?
Who is in charge of the clock in the ghetto?
After Einstein? After Freud? After Mahler?
Did you really think they would burn your papers?
Or your sisters? Or your tribe?

Benjamin Thinking, 1940

Here on the Franco-Spanish border, a man walks in and out of luck—
they've closed the hilltop pass he needs to cross from nightmare
to hope. He's lost his library of children's books,
their lightly printed plates tinted sky-blue and pink, like ribbons
of icing on a child's birthday cake, left behind in Paris trunks
and crates, his passion for collecting dust. He sits in Portbou lamenting
how a few improperly stamped papers have placed him...no-where
exactly, just one more German-speaking Jew stranded without an oven
for his head when the Viennese cut off the gas for non-payment;
how Kafka would have laughed!
He looks at the pills, grateful the trinity of guards in his hotel
are inefficient, fascists like his father, none of them proof enough
against a writer's wishes. The doctor will say his heart gave out,
declare it no sin and bury him Catholic in an unmarked grave,
like all those baptized children who never saw their parents again.
At least his friends have saved his papers: letters on Kafka and Proust,
notebooks he filled while strolling French arcades, his addiction to quotes.
Well, no more walking—he's stuck in a town he doesn't know
and must stay in his room—is it Republican or does it belong to Franco?
Once home in any century but his own, he's obviously made a mistake;
one more look at his watch and he's done.

A Picasso Portrait: Max Jacob

Why would any Jew convert,
freed as he is of the face of God,
when all the world is his monastery,
and something as familiar and dark
as daylight
contains the Lord?

It was a dream perhaps
or an opium pipe he smoked
that made him do it—
after all those years of flinching
in the face of death—
like the faun of Catalonia.

When the end came
(he was still a Jew—
ask any German)
his masses and novenas could not save him
from the ashes,
and even his friend would not save him;

"Dead and gone"
cried the faun of Catalonia,
who never painted him again.

Final Villanelle

I dreamt the dense transparency of snow
was on my eyes, pupils wide open, afraid
of the night and its wavering purple glow:

terror hung like a fog in a deep field below
and fell on the tracks hammered and laid
in the dense transparency of snow.

Strange music greets the trains as they slow—
worms through slats while an orchestra plays
and dances in the wavering purple glow,

in a fire lit by *kapos* to make the darkness grow.
I choke on the ash and my tongue turns gray
with the dense transparency of snow.

If this dream is false and my sweat only for show,
most of us born too late to pray or be preyed
on, why am I chilled by the wavering purple glow?

Better deny or forget and drift in the flow
of lies and myth: no children's brigade
marched out in the dense transparency of snow,
no faces were lit by its wavering purple glow.

Veiled And Unveiled

The wheat field we pass
on the drive to the cemetery
recalls a sour biblical metaphor
and van Gogh's last canvas
found on his easel
after he'd shot himself
dazed by the shadows of crows
overhead.

Near my uncle's grave,
a pair of cenotaphs stands
engraved with the names
of those who disappeared,
among them my grandparents
Moshe and Rivka,
and my father's sisters,
Judith, Rachel and Leah,
names I've never heard him speak
except from the Bible.
Now he reads them weeping,
his left hand resting on the Hebrew,
the other pointing at me,
its index finger, like God's
leaning into my brow.

On the stelae, it says
"Slaughtered and burned by the Germans,"
slaughtered *and* burned;
because they knew
that death was not enough
to excise memory or steal a name.

When we unveil my uncle's stone,
it shines like a bride's face
held in the hands of her father—
a covering up, a taking away
veiled and unveiled at once,
naked like our eyes before an enemy.

Uncle Rudi

—after Gerhard Richter, 1965

Based on a family snap the artist's uncle stands a warrior posed in grand regalia, facing the camera head on, two columns of buttons front his winter coat, its smeared eagles and almost invisible lightning bolts on the collar and epaulets, a swastika perched on his cap. Smiling like an aristocrat, Rudi casually holds a glove in his left hand. Good posture: he's as stiff as a chimney or lighthouse, his face a smirking beacon lit in the gray fog. Behind him a wall of stacked stone and beyond that his hat edges into a tree blurred like smoke and a government ministry, windows arrayed in Bauhaus rows. A few months after this photo was made Rudi's dead at the front, a true believer to the end, as was Richter's father and some other members of the family, their war-time artifacts retired to a box the artist discovers by accident. He might have destroyed the evidence—especially that black and white resemblance he bears in the nose and mouth—but pins their features to the canvas as precisely as he can before loading a brush with turpentine, smearing his almost photographic copy in violation or a personal twist on history or the power of a lens to lose the focus of everything but his uncle's fatal smile.

Coyotes In Connecticut

My father thinks there are coyotes
in Connecticut; says he can tell
by the flattened grass where they sleep
on his lawn, the blunted spears
down at the water's edge
and the parched smell of their coats.
A young neighbor warns him
not to nap alone,
his sandaled toes posing too tempting a snack
for coyotes hiding in the brush.
He worries he doesn't know them—
has never watched a Western movie
or climbed a rock in Arizona;
thinks it's too late to learn
how they howl at the moon
or see them hunt like small dogs
in packs, their shapely teeth glistering.
Years after the last good war
he mistakes them in their camouflage,
forgets how he knew them when
they marched with uniforms in Prague.

BEATING

They let me bleed on what passed for a bridge
in Brooklyn then, a concrete arch over a highway,
my skullcap poised like a black mushroom
on the pavement, my books scattered beyond my arm.

They call it a beat down—someone hits you
so hard and so often you never forget it
or else, if they use your head for a tambourine
you can't recall the beating at all.

That day God must have had an aching back
or tired feet; like when Job called out to Him
begging for some relief from his pain,
and God, having had a bad day of his own

struck out, got angry, like a father whose child
can't get it right: which hand holds the fork,
which fraction is turned upside down
when you divide.

Even today, I recall my body stuttering to a stop,
not getting home on time; my father waiting.
as the gray afternoon lost its light. I told him
I was afraid to move but too stubborn to pass out.

THE GIFT THAT KEEPS ON GIVING

—paper "is the enemy of oblivion", Cassiodorus

Seven decades on the Germans wait two years to tell us
there's one more Matisse in the world, one more Chagall,
and a Franz Marc horse we knew nothing about, a part

of almost 1500 works discovered in a Munich flat,
the Gurlitt horde of Degenerate Art, passed from father to son
like a secret handshake or gold bars in a Swiss bank.

Their rightful owners dead, long-exiled, burned or gassed,
the theft outlives its victims. When the news arrives in time
for my birthday, the third generation's already old

and plenty of lawyers still thrive in German-speaking lands.
Some in the British press see restitution as mere money
for greedy Jews. *Aren't they ever satisfied*, the Bavarians cry,

what more do they want? We want them back, our murdered dead,
our culture, every erased memory. Just tell me where they're buried,
give me their names and you can keep the Matisse like a medal.

LECH LECHA (לֶךְ לְךָ)

—to the land that I will show you

Go, go, go for yourself from the land, from your relatives,
from your father's house, from your past.

Fifty years ago today I set out, a small knit cap on my head,
the curve of my skull echoed
in the great bowl of Talmud Torah's dome
on Coney Island Avenue.

I am creeping up on Abraham, almost as old as he was
in Lech Lecha, my Torah portion, ready to set off with Lot
and Sarah, and all their wealth, and *the souls they had made*
in Haran, the place they were leaving for Canaan.

The souls they had made, not their children,
the sweet little bodies they'd held and washed, kissed and fed;
it's the souls they had made that are taken.

But Sarah and Abraham had no children then, only servants
and converts, those who were ready to follow them
into the wilderness. Perhaps the servants or Lot had the children.

I'm stuck in the text, unclear as to the referent implied
by the noun phrase and its definite article: *the souls*,
a little like Joyce in *The Dead*, looking around at everyone.

Did God mean for them to take their own souls,
Lot's and Sarah's and Abraham's, the ones they had made
for themselves, sojourning in a foreign land?

Fifty years ago this day, I gave a little speech about the awe I felt
standing before the Ark and speaking directly to God.
It was prettily done, without humility and without fear.

But now I am counting souls, those made and unmade,
those given and withheld, in the land to which I've been taken. Or led.

An American Refugee On Vacation In Prague

Summer solstice in the Staré Město of Prague—
everyone as usual looking for Kafka.
Even the 14th Count of Lobkowicz,
a cultured soul who shows me
the 400 year old mummified arm in the Church of St. James,
who speaks of the Master Theodoric
with the voice of a true connoisseur, to whom
locating Tycho Brahe's tomb
in Our Lady Before Týn is the merest child's play,
even he can't find Kafka.
Reported sightings at No.2 and No.3 Celetná
go unconfirmed; the café
at The House of the Black Madonna is closed.

Waiting for more reliable information
I smoke three Havana cigars:
a Romeo and Juliet, a Cohiba and a Partagas.
I do not manage to visit more than two houses in which
Kafka wrote or worked.
I do manage to visit the Castle that gave him nightmares.
I watch the clock on the Jewish Town Hall tower
run the wrong way round
and the Czechs lean backwards going down
the steep escalator in Republiky's Metro.
I do not twist my ankle on the cobbles in Celetná Street;
I do have dinner with two actors in a barrel-vaulted restaurant
two stories below the Gothic ground.
I make love to one woman and to this golden city.
I deserve nothing of this but the sound of bells.

What Do Little Children Know?

We know what the little children know
from the permanent exhibit at the Pinkas synagogue
and the 80,000 names on its walls:

How to paint a watercolor of empty tables
full of hunger;
how to carve a Chanukah lamp from the broken slat
of a freight car;
how to hold a memory in a numbered valise;
how to sculpt an Indian head from a clothespin
and a last potato.

One hour north of the New Jerusalem
the table was never filled, the lamp never lit
the dream of Palestine remained only drips in a paint box.

They could not imagine a future
as we cannot imagine the past,
its weathered stones scattered like broken teeth outside.

At La Provence

Nothing with sour cream or paprika
on the blackboard behind your head
where plats du jour are listed in French
and English on Štupartská street in Prague.

We sit by an open frame window
inhaling the scene, young women in tees
and bare midriffs, their dates with sleeves
rolled up like Brando's in the Fifties.

Shuttered windows and cobbles
are all that remain of Babel's gray dream
of revolution. We sit looking out at these kids
looking back with the wish of an entrée

into a life of luxe, calme et voluptué; they
will learn to work the system. It's given us
this night closing down our former lives
like a curtain, everyone French, all American.

PRAGUE SUITE

1.

Each summer day, thousands of tourists stand and watch
the skeleton on the old astronomical clock
rattle his hour glass in mortal warning
while an unbelieving Moor near-by shakes his carved head

and the clock on the Jewish town hall tower runs backward
to go forth; the Stone Bell never rings.
What city tells time like Prague?
In perfect stasis it measures its minutes in faggots and flames:

Jan Hus will burn forever in the Old Town Square, Kafka
prospectively smells Jan Palach afire with gas, and Mozart sings
in every street, his Stone Guest a perfect Golem.
It's as if God had banished worms and maggots with a spell,

the city as heavenly banquet. At Vladislav's Powder Gate,
where Gothic leans on Art Nouveau, love runs long, renews.

2.

As if he were deaf to the chimes of his Prophets and Saints,
Prague's town counselors plucked out their clockmaker's eyes,
afraid Jan Hanuš would take his magic to Vienna.
From 1450 on, Prague Time ran free, fluid as a river:

the farmers read their Bohemian hours in Arabic numerals, saw
the present in Roman, the past as a Zodiac in a blue Babylonian sky.
No wonder Einstein first lectured on bent time in this place,
spoke at No.2, where Kafka's parents lived and kept him to his books,

or that Kafka felt the world so strange, confronted with this Clock.
From the steps of the Stone Ram, each time he left
Berta's literary salon, Kafka watched its grim Apostles chase
a medieval Jew dressed as Greed; and because he knew

the letters on the ghetto clock ran the other way, K. left his mark
on almost every shop in the town square and wrote 'time cancelled.'

3.

Late in life, I dip a toe in the Now, like Aurelius
feel the past already closing like a river
behind locks, the present tide rising into the future.
How little we know; I make a photo of the tombstones

shuffled like cards in the old Jewish cemetery,
falling every which way beneath the linden trees,
a sea of shipwrecked deaths in golden air;
my snap unknowingly catches a glimpse

of those who are next, tourists walking the winding lane
in the eruv of the dead, where my Father's fathers lie
twelve layers deep to a great astronomer,
a biblical scholar, a social beauty of rank, and Rabbi Löw

who used Prague's clay to make the first Frankenstein.
How brave of us who live without hope of paradise!

4.

O comical monster mirrored in me and mine,
O deathless warrior designed to save Prague's Jews
from the Emperor, is it true you survive in this attic,
a stone tablet placed in your mouth, language as magic?

If so, awake and know we were half-killed
while you slept, feel our pain twitch deep in your thalami
like a phantom limb discharging its grievance
in absent fingers—air clutching air, ineffectual as feet

dancing beneath the gallows; forgive your master Löw,
who stored you too soon in the rafters of the Old-New Shul,
himself equally worshipped and reviled by the gentiles
as either the city's rabbi or an ungodly magician

more feared than his creature. His finger erased God's name
on your forehead, and Frankenstein rested.

5.

Crazy enough to walk all the way down
Neruda Street (from which the poet took his name)
and embassy row, I pass the House of the Three Violins,
St. Nicholas Church and the Kampa,

a small island or peninsula perched
on the northern bank of the Vltava,
where a weir of giant bolted logs awaits,
the entire mechanism shaped like an egg slicer.

It strives to slow the river current down
as a raft of tour boats course around
its near end, and my two souls sweat with the effort
of acknowledging a trans-Atlantic loss:

how an American Jew who's no longer Czech,
discovers a bicameral self in late middle age.

6.

The ancient Bridge rejects you, pushes you away,
you on your tired legs; how can it stand over water
seven hundred years without feeling the need to give in
to gravity, fall to its knees like you?

Today, the arches look new; the afternoon sun in its pity
washes the ancient pillars anew, cleanses the stone saints,
and lights up the golden letters forced on a Jew
who paid many crowns to announce the error of his ways

in Hebrew. No bombs fell on this city and Charles built well:
from his old Town Square to the university,
from his bridge to the castle where Kafka's nightmares still tremble.
And above them all, the cathedral spires floating in the air

shimmering in the heat, dissolving the tangible.
It's almost real; you stand on a bridge to nowhere and smile.

7.

In Wenceslas Square, I came not for the saint but the martyr.
Behind the old king on his charger
a parasol of rays blinds me, making pictures impossible.

Downstream, in that first block between the Hotel Europa
and the king's statue, no eternal flame's been placed,
not even a plaque; only a bed of flowers spotted with trash.

It's so hot I've missed the buried cross marking the spot
where he set himself afire and fell; by the time Palach burned
Martinů was ten years dead and I too young to know

his Field Mass for Lidice or the shootings in the forest.
Today his music's sad plaint plays in my head, clears my memory
of Soviet tanks. Prague's freedom is some consolation for his death

but not enough. In this strange space not remotely a square
time bends to near-silence; where is the echo, where is the shout?

8.

Each death is a wound the world closes up
with endless renewal, knits invisible sutures
in mindless amplitude,
erases by leaving behind

rivers of ingratitude, patched with mud and indifference.
How grim to think like this and slake one's soul
with statistics, all history conceived *en masse*
a sociology of signs, in dollars and otherwise,

how ignorant to believe there will ever be another Will
like Stratford's or an accidental Einstein.
Death dresses the world in its motley of change,
throws up the great

like a plow in a harrow or a shark in a wave,
engineers millions of ends to make us one clay.

First Love

—for M.M. (1931-2013)

My older cousin Magda who knew Mengele
who made me home-fried potatoes
just like my mother's and my mother's mother.

My first cousin Magda who had a dark helmet of hair
and a great bosom the shape of Europe
filled with the milk of Europe and its acid.

My cousin Magda who tasted of tears, always
with the soul of a Hungarian gypsy grieving
for a twisted son she never bore.

And cousin Magda who married Tibor who cut
garments for chairs and couches in the Fifties
upholstering America with his simple hopes.

And especially because my cousin Magda loved
my father more than anyone else the esteemed uncle
who'd rescued her brother from the cauldron.

That cousin Magda was the queen of woe
and her easy anger saved her for a while.
I never caught up with any of her worries but one—

I removed a tumor from her brain and she died
twenty years later and was twenty years older than I am.
So we never wed; and this was Magda's only luck.

FROM
SHADES & GRACES: NEW POEMS
(2020)

Ten Reflections
On Ramón Gómez De La Serna (1888-1963)

I

He has the eyes of a tightly-sewn button

With the pupils of a cat and the face of a bear
He climbs into my bed when I am dreaming.
I see a new reality through a single thread.

II

Up among the stars there isn't a single nightingale

Even in the dark
A free bird needs oxygen to sing.

III

The q is the p coming back from a walk

Like you I have lived my life backwards
Old when I was young and young when I am old.
You left Madrid and I left New York.
I drink in the backwaters of my new ancient city.

IV

The peacock is a retired myth

Shoot if you must a parliament of owls
Or else retire all thirteen ways of looking at a blackbird.
But do not expunge our faith in feathers, I pray you:
Set up a windbreak or spray a peacock with water if it cries;
Put it in a box at night and give it a radio, silence.

V

The silk scarf is the goodbye of a caress

What a tragedy! Her hands grew old and her rings didn't.
Eighteen when you met and she thirty-eight,
Carmen de Burgos smelled of cigarettes and perfume and age.
She brought you the comedy of a century.
You felt like a hundred when "Colombine" left you Ramón
but in her scarf was the scent of a bird and your greguerías.

VI

The hardest fish to catch is soap in water

This is why you never washed
and called your first novel *The Unlikely Doctor.*

VII

At night on a lonely train we travel with two women: the one with us
and the one reflected in the glass

There are at least two possibilities:
This is how she looked when you were both young
Or how someone else looked then or looks now.
In any case you must not share this memory with your companion
Since it is certain she already knows.

VIII

Doors get angry with the wind

At the sound of Franco's advice
You leave for Argentina with your Jewish wife.
Even a surrealist must get real at times.

IX

Fragrance is the flowers' echo & The moon is the porthole of night

A word meaning hubbub or babble of sound turned into lyrical
aphorism.
Does "Humor + Metaphor = Greguería"?
Is it inscribed on your tombstone?

X

The moon of the skyscrapers is not the same as the moon of the
horizon

The world depends on aspiration and point of view.
Sometimes low-lying fruit is the highest reward and the pinnacle
loses
its value by reflection.
We live in the sky but breathe in the shadows
Where low is high and high is low.

[The titles of sections I-IV, VI-VII, and line two in V are Gomez de la
Serna greguerias translated by Bill Zavatsky]

THE THREE WEISSES

Shades and graces come in threes: my cousins in Queens
were aunt and uncle to me,
the first I knew as elderly
rich with sandpapered faces
and thin-rimmed glasses they wore like monocles.

My first lesson in the upper classes—
a tinted portrait above the mantle
where Hettie and Syd and Uncle Carl were posed as kids
in white smocks with puffy sleeves
big as their heads, and a favorite spaniel for color.

Upstairs their sentient mother lived in solitary splendor,
my father's Aunt Rose, already a hundred
when I was five, whose backside routinely greeted me
freshly bathed and powdered
with a faint smell of garlic and uric acid in Queens.

Syd's husband I never knew
or can't remember, and soon after he died
she moved back in with the other two
and seemed as much a spinster as they ever did,
eternally wed to brother and sister.

Of the past not a word was spoken—
one could never know how Hettie's young heart
had been broken or why Carl with a smile like Coolidge
never pursued a bride
or wore sweaters in summer until the day he died.

THE DUKE OF FLATBUSH

—Edwin Donald Snider, 1926-2011

We were five and six: the summer bliss
of Bensonhurst, its flowing grass in our noses,
dandelions waving their yellow manes,
the smell of dirt in the outfield.

It was only a name, *Duke*, a talisman
of greatness, repeated under my breath
each time I took a swing,
my softly rounded body sturdy on its legs.

Duke, Jeffrey yelled, as he lofted a pitch,
clapping when I punched my way through the air
and the Spaldeen flew
like a satellite launched in haze.

The Duke of Flatbush died today
and something closed. A tassel torn free
from a valve in my heart flapped like old laundry
in its gutter of blood.

My head ached. How many days had passed
from that last soft-toss session
to the morning I stood and fell at my bedside,
the virus lodged in lumbar number five

claiming my legs? A year later, I would partially rise—
like Duke—*my lightness of bearing couldn't disguise
my darkness of being*—like Duke living his life
in the shadow of Willie and Mick.

In The E.R.

In the E.R. we stab the lung
with a scalpel like a small harpoon,
sometimes the blood comes spurting out
sometimes the face swells up like a moon.

We spit them out, the cyclist who hits
a pit without his helmet on,
the toy boy who crosses against the green
his I-Pod blasting *You Be Cool*.

I miss the rushing through the halls.
I miss the whining of the saws.
I miss the drama of Shock and Trauma.
I miss the blooding of my claws.

Not All Will Heal

Every intern knows it doesn't matter how long an incision is,
just how wide: one stitch placed the same as its neighbor—
a cut doesn't heal along its length
but side to side. We close wounds as fast as we can,
before blood and fibrin clot
thread in the gaps like bridges of rope crossing a ravine.

A wound too wide for silk festers in time—
its edges turn red with grunge in days,
and depths go gray. A belly or chest agape like that
needs wire to snug its lips together, trusting they will kiss
like lovers on a screen, fingers stretched
against the window of a train that's left.

Time's not enough for some wounds. Fixing a nose
never the same as closing a belly,
tying a silk not like twisting a wire.
Pull too hard on a stay and the tubing bruises like a punch,
tears the skin and the dog-eared scar
marks a patient for years. You've signed your name in a way

even God can't erase; closed but open like a grave.

H.M., The Man Without A Memory

—1926-2008

He knew his name, that much
he could remember,
also the stock market crash in 1929, a war and such,

but otherwise time was gone, sundered
after seizure surgery
locked him in an eternal December

for more than half a century.
Each day the same meal and the same guest
greeted with the same glee,

as if never before seen, each a quotidian test
of his special deficit.
So each time was the first time, an infinite jest

withstood with quiet eloquence. Unlit
by any doubt, his inability to form new memories
protected him from history's ugliest bits:

no glib suits as president, no thin tea.
Embarked at twenty-seven
on a major "career" of discovery,

Henry Molaison, known to us all as H.M.
died in Windsor Locks at 82,
his brain as mysterious as Zen.

In the biology of memory his was the best clue
(before PET scans arrived and MRI)
for two different systems of learning, one true

to name and place in his lost hippocampi,
the other for riding a bike or jumping a trace—
there in his thalamus and motor nuclei

lay a legacy he couldn't erase.

On The Anniversary Of The Moon Landing

Forty years ago today I stood in a sick children's ward,
a green paper cap on my head,
watching a man take a flickering step
off a ladder. Nothing else we've done since seems as good.

The anchorman exclaiming in childish joy
might have been speaking for me three months before,
as I stood on the bottom step of a spiral staircase
on Bay State Road, watching you descend

in bouffant sleeves and a glowing orb of hair—
my first look and a lunar landing of another kind.
I write these words three days after Cronkite died
and no one's gone back to the moon in decades,

the other side dark and barely known.
A week after that epochal landing we entered
into our own mystery—and voyaging on Love
I'm still amazed to see you turn your face to me.

That September, You Remember 1975

The Manhattan sky filled
with smoky clarity,
my young wife and I mounting
Broadway's first escalators,
the new Uris Theater opening
with Count Basie and his band
putting out some roaring Bop
and Ella scatting her way
to intermission.
               And after the break,
Old Blue Eyes came out
and almost brought our breathing
to a stop:
thrown flowers and a glass
of brown scotch sat at the piano
next to a rose, coiling inside itself
the gray smoke he'd blown
between sets.
             We were two
of two thousand
perched in his palm
listening to every last phrase
of our favorite song,
and when the last notes
of that long lonesome road
drifted away, sat shocked
to see her come back out and sing duets
with the man, holding hands just like us
as if they too were still young.

That Stinking Rose Of Garlic

As doomed love is better than lovelessness,
all the sensible world loves this stinking rose
better than no rose at all.

In the old places and the old times
women slept with garlic hung
between their breasts like a lantern of desire
and the men breathed its aroma like a stone
laced up with vines.
                              Wanting slapped at their sides
as a wave does on the chine of a sloop
or a horse flicking its tail in the rain.

Even a few cloves popped on the tongue
would keep inconstant lovers away
or drive the vampires of New York and San Francisco
back into the darkness.

After eating some garlic last night,
its bulbs pressed to romance Italian scallops and pasta,
conjure aioli, or dress the slaughtered cattle of Kansas,
I slept uneasy dreaming of sleep
and when I awoke the old nickel sky felt like rain.

I've rubbed it raw on matzos, a trick my father taught me,
and felt memory bend to its power: a sweet bitterness
shared with its close relations,
alkali and belladonna—
O garlic, leaf and flower, we dream and die.

SHOWING THE APARTMENT

I blame no one for walking out—
the obvious paintings on the walls,
the crazed cookie jar with its hint
of chinoiserie,
the usual prints with their tired Parisian views.

If you've come for nothing, welcome—
there's nothing here, not even the news

of how he lived his life.

Evidently, he looked from the prospect
of this park into an unmoored century
and one credible subject

beauty.
Perhaps you too find that unacceptable.

THE LOST NOTEBOOK

Some lines on neutrinos, weightless and uncharged,
storming through our bodies by the millions
painlessly wounding us at speeds as great as light,

and how incompatible equations for dark matter, dark energy
and gravity bind our lives together
in ordinary incomprehensible ways.

A few words about entering a tabernacle,
the biggest I'd seen, walls hung with seven species of fruit,
ripening gourds, and strings of glass crystals shining against the sky,

the broken shards of mirrors covered in a house of mourning.
My father's death at last year's harvest time
has me looking at the ceiling with wonder,

perhaps as he does, the stars in his bones and him in the stars.
So much for drafts that never got revised,
and one or two ideas forever contained in the well

of unstable memory,
its fluidic darkness extinguishing each one like a match.
This much and so little lost in a few pages, a year's worth set

in calf leather, tanned black and bought by my wife in a shop
on the Grand Canal.
Always too rich for me—I never liked its heft

or the fancy straps used to tie its covers shut.
I must have meant to share it with a stranger, every page but
the endpaper hiding my pen's snug quiver.

ALIEN

One day they move far off into
another part of your head—
it's as if they'd died.

Your eyes don't meet,
their trains don't run on your tracks,
their streetcars take different streets.

They think they're Arcturians
from a blue planet. Beliefs become reality.
Next thing you know

they move to San Francisco
and paint their faces blue
at Burning Man in the desert.

You may find there's nothing left
for art to save, no drug or suture
capable of healing their hearts. Worse

sitting in the next room, miles apart
you don't even know how it happens
but they insist they tell you.

THE OLD BOAT

Motoring back in the haze, the Bay Bridge
and three remaining microwave towers
at Whitehall Bay invisible,
I steer towards their girdled steel
navigating like a bird
the magnet in my head receiving signals.

How much longer can I sail
this brutal way, in an open boat
going a few miles a day? She's getting on
for a boat but young for a person—
twenty years old and still in Bristol shape,
her lines and bright work bringing stares

as she lies at anchor, my wife
and I hardly worth a wave
from younger sailors passing astern.
Artists have no solitary claim to such beauty—
Rembrandt's *Storm on the Sea of Galilee*
and Turner's sunsets

mere rehearsals in Plato's cave,
a dumb show of perfect shapes and silent
poetry. My old boat's nose rises to a real ocean
and falls the same to age, like a sunflower alive
and glowing, her head bent to the wind
and the coming hour.

What's Left Out

What's left out
between the lines
in the white space
between the words
is more important
than thought
or belief, even
more important
than facts or the truth
you kick with a shoe
into the street.

What's left out
makes reality
condense like vapor
in a stew pot, that savor
of paprikash, of salt
and cinnamon
on your tongue
the taste of heaven
misplaced in childhood
reclaimed
with the coming of age.

The Drone

From ten thousand feet it watches and waits,
a sharpshooter with a heart of oil.

From ten thousand feet death opens its door,
levitates like a cloud of dust in Sodom

until finding the merchant in his souk
and the passengers in their car

with a suddenness, addictive and sure,
God's hand rests and smites them all.

QUANDARIES & LIES

—the closest planet to the Sun, possesses a lot of ice,
NYT, November 30, 2012

Erasmus says you must arrange your face
each morning before leaving your door—
wear one mask for friends, the least
contentious, another for the rich or the poor.

Even planets mutate their faces—
immensities dwell in the smallest places:
close to the Sun Mercury seethes
on its equator at 800 degrees

but deep in its polar caves the planet remains
as cold as space,
and ice of purest water crazes
its youngest craters.

Could there be more temperate burrows
where Mercury's ice has vaporized
so that organic molecules
and life itself may arise
from a chance encounter of comet and crust?

Who knows? The universe of souls like the skies
seems a concatenation of quandaries and lies.
Beneath the warmest smile
a countenance may disguise

deep hostility or a lack of surprise.

MEDULLOBLASTOMA

I hear you're writing a thesis
on the deaths of children expressed in poems.
Perhaps you haven't seen them die yourself
and if you did might forego the subject.

I'm writing to tell you how
the crusts of their scalps become very dry
after chemo and the tiny hairs left behind
curl like watch springs.

They are the first to know—
their eyes glimmering with knowledge.
It's useless to tiptoe around their beds
to whisper and tell them lies.
Their dying is slow
and they see it from a long way off.

OF WANTING THERE'S NO END

—Arshile Gorky (1904-1948)

In two self-portraits made from memory
Gorky sits on his mother's knee decades after
the Ottoman Turks starve her to death.
He came to America to forget and married Agnes
who gave him a family; he painted all the time—

but never them. Imagine that last year and a half
when the studio burned down and he lost his work:
he had to shit in a bag from the cancer in his colon,
broke his neck and paralyzed his arm in a car wreck,
and Matta, that Chilean wretch, screwing his wife.

Vostanik Adoyan lied about everything he could:
his name, his age, his nationality. So deranged
he wanted to be Russian instead of Armenian,
wanted to be brave like Achilles and crack wise
like Maxim Gorky. Wanted, wanted, wanted.

So he went to the barn in back and scrawled in chalk
"Farewell my beloveds" on a box, hanging himself
with his good hand on a lamp cord, eyes feasting
one last time on fiery plants, upright cocks and lobster claws
in combat; and saw at once it was more than enough.

No Wires, No Shackles

—Ross Douthat, NYT, April 15, 2012

The man with the Google glasses wakes-up
in a comfortable, full-service cage,
brews some coffee and goes out into the world
where everything he needs appears on his lenses
like magic: the weather, his calendar,
messages from friends, the virtual map of a virtual city.

A rat navigating a maze
he makes his effortless way,
photographs anything he's told to,
buys what they whisper in the temples of his frames.

When he thinks of the one he loves
her face suddenly appears at the bottom of his bifocals.
She smiles at the sunset he sends her by video
and waves. He's befriended dozens just like her
but can't remember her name.

The man with the Google glasses
never guesses someone else sees what he sees,
every thought recorded and reported in full,
no one knows him better than this stranger.

Churchill said
a lie gets half way around the world
before the truth gets out of bed in the morning;
now it goes all the way to the moon. Bandwidth.

They will take care of you, cradle to grave
as we go sliding, not deciding towards something
that looks like freedom but is only fake.
To the man with the Google glasses
the real that *is* is not; what else has slithered away?

MOBTOWN

I.

They planned to kill him right here,
not far from Latrobe's Merchants Exchange,
torn down in 1901, a giant market and custom house,
where only ten thousand came in two hours
to view his remains, a hint of a smile
playing on his lips like soot
on a darkened candle. At nearby Calvert Station
Lincoln's casket was placed on a bier and closed
for the train ride to Springfield, hawkers split
over two sides of an unsettled question
sold *his* portrait for a dime and his killer's for a quarter.

North and south of Baltimore, almost no one remembers this;
losing in games is almost all we know.

II.

An old Southern town, Baltimore grew outward from the water,
each ring circling the harbor like regret. At its center
the first casualties of Rebellion died.
They built Oriole Park near Calvert Station
to make the city seem new and halted construction
when green shards of glass and rotting planks
were dug up in the outfield grass
and pored over like holy relics discovered
the family bar of George Herman Ruth.

III.

Resentments great and small built this town—
we hate the team Ruth played for
and that uniform he wore inscribed in script
with an old enemy's name in blue.

The trains no longer run on Pratt and Eutaw Streets,
the Station's been embalmed as a museum of sports.
Out beyond the outfield wall an ugly modern box
shaves our view of Baltimore's downtown towers
and further beyond the Block and its girly bars have shrunk
like a customer's cock in the cold.

South of New York we think we live in a city outside of history,
losing in games is all we know.

MENDACITY

To *mend* is at the center of it, to make whole the rip in the world
by stitching it up with lies; there are never enough
for all the rents and hollowness, the empty caverns
of unpleasant facts. Menelaus, that ancient king,
had need of lies as smooth as Helen's back,
his family's adultery, incest and cannibalism
much on his mind, his own wife's faithlessness and the war...
    And not just kings but scribes
who wish the world were otherwise,
    and make it so with lies.

FROM FATHER SLEEPING

Locus coeruleus, the blue spot in the brain
where a bright dot of pigment controls our mortal waking,
where all that raveled coil's unraveled by day
and we greet the sunshine as fate, kismet burning.
The legends say *no tears for the dying*
lest you impede them on their way to heaven,
my eyes so dry at your bedside they cancel my yearning
that you stay. For this boy
father's the prime subject, his approval joy
and all else dross.
The only history the boy knows is in this body,
its loss definitively loss.

ii

Kidneys still working, a silenced monitor and soft sweet breaths
make almost no sound in the universe.
Days go by with only moments of agitation
that slump into rest
and the rare round of grunts in a language of mystery and allusion,
half Hungarian, half Venusian,
as if lungs so far underwater
could manage only deeply aquatic words
like a whale feeling its way to a distant shore.

Restfully he lies beyond distress, never sick
for more than three days at a time.
How could this happen he asks
not yet oblivious to his rapid decline
nor fooled by our hopes for his recovery.
That's how you made ninety-nine, I reply
but the past six weeks still startle

as if Death were a grim German soldier who'd come
to his hiding place and noted the mark of the Jew on his face.

We try shaking him awake but forego the pain
I once gave my patients: the thumbnail pinch, the sternal rub
and stiffly watch others stick him with probes as if
there's finally an answer to life's indignity.
No dear friend, mentor in all things, there's no alternative.
Let go your stiff arm, the bent leg release.

iii

> *Locus coeruleus: a small rod-shaped nucleus located within the dorsal wall of the rostral pons and lateral floor of the fourth ventricle, a part of the brain stem; sixteen mm long and 5 mm wide, the LC contains about 20,000 cells. The nucleus is the principal site for synthesis of norepinephrine in the brain. Melanin granules inside the medium-sized neurons of the LC contribute to its blue color; it is thereby also known as the nucleus pigmentosus pontis, meaning "heavily pigmented nucleus of the pons." ...*
>
> *Norepinephrine from the LC has an excitatory effect on most of the brain, mediates arousal and primes the brain's neurons to be activated by stimuli. The locus coeruleus receives inputs... allowing emotional pain and stressors to trigger chemical responses. It also gets inputs...which integrate[s] autonomic and environmental stimuli...The locus coeruleus may be involved in clinical depression, panic disorder, and anxiety. Some antidepressant medications act on neurons in the LC. The locus coerulius is intimately involved in REM sleep and dreaming: the dream in prose.*

iv

When the dreamer's in his dream, like the dancer in his dance,
he can't tell what's real outside from the reality within.
He knows he's dreaming but it doesn't matter;
the LC's firing and his arms move without volition,
eyelids twitch, his penis rises and his heart races with a thrill.

When my father's sleeping perhaps he's dreaming of me
like I am of him. Then we are both as real as a sunrise
in the mind of the other.
Perhaps I'm the dream he's been having all this last century
and he will be the dream I am having next year.

Danto thought Warhol a philosopher as much as artist
because his Brillo Box seemed as real as the box
on a supermarket shelf; no visual evidence could disprove
what the artist claimed, hence an end to *retinal art* as Duchamp proclaimed.
If I'm not the son he wished for, how would my father know?

He dreamed me up so I appear at his bedside, like a genie
watching the sheets blow with each breath. Dying is slow.

vi

When I was a young doctor we called it *sundowning*,
watching grief and disorientation descend with darkness,
the formerly meek and gentle getting loud and violent,
the old afraid of their lostness as if PTSD came out at night.

My father at night is the not the same man I know by day,
his inner Kurz comes out in a shadow land of foreign shores
and prisons. Up every hour to pee, he shouts for help,
fearing he'll fall to the ground or into the hole of his other self.

Agitated by fear, not knowing where he is or why,
he curses his wife and nurses as Nazi jailers.
What life he has by day disappears as the sun goes down.
I call him too late and he refuses to talk to his son,

the first break between our souls in sixty years,
the first brick laid in the permanent wall to come.

viii

> *The role of the locus coeruleus in cognitive function in relation to*
> *stress is complex and multi-modal. Norepinephrine released from*
> *the LC in the right amount acts to increase working memory....*
> *Opioids inhibit the firing of neurons in the locus coeruleus. When*
> *opioid consumption is stopped, the increased activity of the locus*
> *coeruleus contributes to the symptoms of opiate withdrawal.*
> *Since the locus coeruleus is the major source of noradrenergic*
> *innervation in the brain and sends widespread connections to*
> *brain areas above...and below it..., restoration of normal LC*
> *function may be of potential therapeutic value for cognition and*
> *respiratory dysfunction. Oh yes, up to 70% of locus coeruleus*
> *neurons are lost in Alzheimer's Disease.*

There it is, death or its simulacrum:
the LC, blue eye of the brain—
my father's hurricane.

THE BLIZZARD
—*i.m. Ilona (1943-2010)*

The boughs hang heavy, discontinuously striped
with little coffins of snow
and great white globules bloom
like poisonous carnations.

These are not the snows of Pissarro
and I am not the boy
who dreamed of riding elegant black carriages
across the purple avenues of Paris.

This is Baltimore where the fractured trees look hellish
and we can't open our doors
against the wet weight of four-foot drifts
and the chilblain cold that blows.

Sometimes it's easier to fly than walk.
All night the snow covered ground
unpacks my sleep, its white light flooding
off the mounds bursts the blinds,

when word comes by phone how you missed a step
at the top of the basement stairs
and broke your fall with your lovely face.
You snapped a rib and collarbone, and blooded the brain

but somehow not your wrists, always thin as bracelets.
They may find the clot in time and if you awake
the world will seem new and uncovered,
almost as if we were young, not melting away.

WHEN BACH WAS STREET

Not all powdered wigs and cantatas. He was young,
had pimples and hormones and undiffused anger.
He made chief organist too early and didn't shut his mouth.
As a teenager it was one church after another.
He was some kind of genius and difficult;
go figure.
He complained about the choir and Rambach,
the choirmaster.
He argued with the bassoonist.
Not ordinary dissing like
you didn't really say what I thought you said
or there's one small punch left in me
and I'm going to knock you flat on your little ass
but one of those twisty German words
with a dozen syllables that called the bassoonist
a nanny-goat or meant
a bassoonist breaking wind after eating a green onion.
Bach often went absent without leave,
like the time he asked for a month
to visit Buxtehude in Lübeck
and took three to walk there and back.
Two hundred eighty miles takes a lot of shoe leather.
In the meanwhile his hero had died, and he thought his daughter
a dog. On his return
the church elders in Arnstadt took a vote and got in Bach's face:
in the minutes, *surprising variations and irrelevant ornaments*
which obliterate the melody
and confuse the congregation
like Coltrane.
They also caught him riffing on his organ for a strange damsel.
Bach was a stud but he'd taken enough of their gas.
He left Arnstadt and married his cousin Anna Magdalena
who had twenty or thirty children all of whom wrote music
and played organ. That man was phat.

GRAFFITI

His shortest best-loved poem, his name,
found on this hill high above Cape Sounio
where the sea god's temple stands on a cliff
between the Aegean and a touristy bay.

On the beaches below no one has declaimed
Childe Harold in years; still they crane to see
his scrawled *B* and the lesser letters trail out
from a dark and veiny wound in the upper block

of the second column to my right.
One can hardly sit anywhere on this rocky plain
without rubbing some name or date,
most the work of anonymous hands

and the autographs of vandals, all weathering the same
hungering for a fame even the god forgot.

THE VICAR

—in memory of John Updike

It was much too cold to snow the day we got the news:
the old vicar had died; not a sound
rose skywards from the trees, their barren pews
half-shorn, the rabbits gone to ground.

A tall attentive bird,
with ruddy face and shock of parson white,
he kept unblinking eyes upon the world
and bookish sermons flowing day and night.

And I the sort of tender boy he said he built them for,
my happy hours spent, a hand upon the spines:
all those small-town woes, with covers blown and torn,
and pages thumbed from use, the record of our times.

Though unappointed at the end, the vicar might have chosen
an icy day like this to leave, silent, sunlit, frozen.

THE MARLED BEAM

—Nicholas Hughes (1962-2009)

In your father's letters, a premonition—
all that boy and man talk about rods and creels,
and the size of King salmon in Alaskan streams.

You fished for grayling as far from the rock
in your mother's heart as possible, but in your chest
its replicon dwelled for years

like a sunken barge, hazardous to navigation.
She called you her precious ruby but left you behind
to go fishing with him—the one art you shared.

What was useful in Ted was no part of your dream—
your wilderness outside, his wildness within.
At one he saw in your eyes a shine like Syl's:

wet jewels, the hardest substance of the purest pain.
Soon after he died you were done with waiting
out by the sedge, at the pottery oven, even pie making,

the tedious things one does to pass time in a cabin.
They find you at home, swung at the edge of life,
the nylon twine holding you tight to its beam.

Vissi D'Arte

There's a lot of operatic ink on the old man in the gym:
on his left scapula, Tosca's *vissi d'arte. vissi d'amore,*
on his right, *please help me to be more beautiful*
and at the flanks, longer inscriptions I've got no time to read.

No barbed-wire bands or vines clasp his arms, no designs at all,
just blue words sitting against his albino skin,
topped by short cropped hair
and a sharply pointed beard neatly trimmed like a devil's.

Soon art and love will begin to sag and what will his surgeon think?
Or the pathologist who flays him or the mortician in his lab floating in
a wave of formaldehyde, like typewriter correcting fluid,
the soul escaping from its dermatological thesaurus

into the wordless ether? What they think will depend
on who they are, their literary or sexual taste. Perhaps
he hopes one will say this was an educated man, a romantic,
a devotee of culture, desperate to hold his art as close as a lover.

Seven Or Eight Reflections
On Erik Satie (1866-1925)

— I breathe carefully, a little at a time

I

When I was Young, People used to Say to Me: Wait Until You are Fifty,
You'll See. I am Fifty. I Haven't Seen Anything.

Some ideas are too big for the average brain to hold
Gravitational waves take too much energy
To think about. Some outlandish things may be true
And some reasonable assertions actually false.
Lives have been wasted on swallowing a mouse
And no house can hold an elephant.
But here's the secret: if you want to store an elephant
In a refrigerator first open the door and remove the giraffe.

II

I Came Into the World very Young, in an Age very Old

Lucky to be young in the world,
Lovely to die before it turns senile or insane,
Before it looks at you with hollow eyes,
Before it speaks
With a snaggle-toothed mouth.

III

Experience is a Form of Paralysis

I am tired of always dying with a broken heart
But I remember Suzanne
The girl who laughed during sex.

Why attack God?
He may be as miserable as we are.
His memory is longer.

IV
Musical Directions

Look at the world *like a nightingale with a toothache,*
There is beauty, there is pain.
You must write as *light as an egg.*
Wonder about yourself, Open your head.
Provide yourself with shrewdness.

The musician is perhaps the most modest of animals,
But he is also the proudest.
It is he who invented the sublime art
Of ruining poetry.

V
Life in the Shape of a Pear

He was born in Honfleur and moved to Paris at four.
It was all downhill from there.
On to Montmartre, then Arcueil,
Always to a smaller room.

He wrote four bars for Valadon, less than half a minute
And never loved again. She was the leaf
At the top of the pear.

VI
I am by Far Your Superior, but my Notorious Modesty
Prevents me from Saying So

A motto for poets.

VII
Memories of an Amnesiac

He died of cirrhosis, in poverty, from too much absinthe.
His apartment was replete with squalor and chaos—
Like life, a clutch of umbrellas and one grand piano
On top of another,
A piano like a post office or columbarium
With parcels and letters.

In the pockets of his velvet suits, lost compositions
The chief of which was *Vexations*.
Who can remember a man who barely forgot
Where his *Dreamy Fish* was stored?

[The seven titles and the lines in italics are aperçu by Satie]

Last Night At The Huguenot House
With The Black Monks Of Mississippi
—for Theaster Gates

The house was singing, the lights in the windows watchful eyes.

The voices were rising, growling, cooing, begging
as if in lullaby.

The house was singing *If I Had a Hammer* and thinking
I could fix myself.

The boards were ringing to *House of The Rising Sun*
and if the house had legs it would have moved to Chicago.

The house said keep on singing:

Sing for the 1700 Huguenots in Kassel who found shelter here.

Sing for the Brothers Grimm.

*Sing for the Kassel Synagogue destroyed in the thirties
and all the souls who died still dreaming
in the sub-camp of Dachau.*

Sing for the civilians who died in this city by aerial bombardment

and sing for the homeless.

*Sing for the soldiers who died by hand-to-hand combat
and the 80th Infantry Division that freed my city.*

So when the Black Monks of Mississippi began singing
Strange Fruit, the house with broken windows and holes
in its ceiling thought to itself
*all of us victims
will stop the bleeding.*

At The Reading I Don't Mean

I don't mean to turn my back on you
like Miles Davis blowing his horn
with bop.

I don't mean to be impolite
like a cat scatting through the garbage
for fried goodies thrown out
a window
after all the limes are squeezed and gone
and the bottles of Corona smashed
into stars.

I don't mean to flex my lats
in your face
or deflect your gaze from my gluts.

I don't mean nothing about posing
my poems this way
but shame on me if they ain't good enough

to blow a hole through your head
setting the top of your tingling spine
ringing
like a gong set free in the wind.

In-Painting

Time has sandpapered this nose too much,
it needs repair: a thin skin
of burnt sienna and turpentine

will do to recapture the murk and shine
of Rembrandtean dark,
that physical mark of a simile

put there by mirror neurons firing
in the artist's brain.
Whatever we call such cellular activity, self-love

or empathy, Rembrandt mastered it
and we have enough to think we see
a face painted by him as real as yours or mine.

This is why a conservator bends at his bench
working for hours—like an infant smiling
or a bird staring into a mirror—

hoping to save each imperfection in a perfect way.
Beauty must have its flaw. He leaves behind
a few bristles trapped in paint.

How The Trick Is Done

Wrapped in chains and padlocks
I hang by my feet in stocks,
before lowering myself down
into gallons of green water
brimming over
an old case of mahogany and steel.

It feels a lot like Houdini's
Chinese Water Torture trick
in which a glass face fronts the audience;
they can see you frown
as if your escape might fail.
Then the curtain comes down
and memory floods in with its useful hints:

how to slip free from a straightjacket
twisting your shoulder out from its socket,
how to spit up a key from a gastric cleft
in order to pick at the locks,
how to shrug off your chains
while holding your breath and climbing your legs.

He had three minutes to do all this
before his unfolded self had to open the stocks.
But *today's trick* isn't *that* trick.
Sure, I've got more time than he did
and no audience. Still,
if I open my mouth, I'll drown.

THE CULT OF BEAUTY

We came ashore at the end of a narrow strait
watching tourists stroll the stony paths
of an outdoor museum

where thirty thousand souls once worshipped and played,
coming together in trade or else the Delian games.
I sweat a drop or two into the sea—

it's noon in beauty's hell and emptiness everywhere.
No one born on Delos was less than a god,
so gravid women were taken off before making a mess.

Even the dead and dying weren't left
but removed to graves off shore
before death might spoil Apollo's perfect realm

with putrefaction. Only his acolytes dwelled
in what they called the brightest spot on earth,
an island like a lens,

where nothing lives today but the past,
its columns and houses in perfect rows,
and five stone lions who guard the sacred lake

in which Apollo rose and his sister's temple sank
without a trace. A single column marks her place
like a bone her brother threw away.

Talking To Mother & Father

I expect I will talk to your graves, why not—
I talk to the cat
and refer to inanimate objects as he's and she's
depending on a hierarchy of needs
and whether I think the book or glass
can talk back when needed to.

It's not encouragement I seek
beyond the reproach of letters unopened and repairs undone
but the reassurance of my voice in the house
and boat, the reply of pipes knocking,
the grumble of washing machines
and the whisper of wind in the rigging.

And when I do I think the voices of the dead
will be louder, more insistent, more like mine.

WINTER POEM

—my last defense/ is the present tense—Gwendolyn Brooks

All that makes us human is so tenuous, even words—
kimono in Japanese means *thing to wear*
but kiwi is the name of a bird or a fruit, an indeterminate
that should be the sound of the bird or the taste on your teeth
in the fruit. Where to begin?
All was darkness before the word and the void opened up
to the light. I don't know where to go at my age but onwards
towards the light and embrace it. Today is someone's birthday
and someone else's anniversary and a day of remembrance.
The yahrzeit candle glows in antithesis.
Even the objects in our home practice denial, pray
for rapture. As long as I can move I am moving up, moving out.
There is no darkness.
I wear a scroll on my forehead, like God's thumb.
I am the scale He is pushing down, weighing
the one hundred foot poplar in my eye, vanishing the scream
in my ear. I come out of my skin, it turns gold,
I come out of my head, it is iron, I come out of love
and silence the birds. Memories slip away. I am reconciled
to my tongue. Silence is the most precious state of being.
So all will be well and nothing will complain.
The low winter sun rakes the field and the room;
in the winter's light I hear the silent growing thing.

IN GRATITUDE

Necessary Speech: New & Selected Poems would not have been possible without the editorial advice of David Bergman, Robert Cooperman, Cortney Davis, and Jennifer Wallace. Many of the New Poems underwent review by these stalwarts before first publication in journals; I am deeply grateful for their critical suggestions. Reducing a lifetime corpus of work is a painful process; nevertheless, the suggestions of friends and colleagues for the excision of a large number of the New Poems and many of the Selected Poems were honored in almost every case.

Many thanks to Terese Svoboda for her kind and imaginative blurb on the back cover, so typical of her own poems. A special salute goes out to Grace Schulman for taking on this task once more. Their fellow blurbist, David Bergman, also authored the extraordinary introductory essay about my literary career in *Shades & Graces*.

As always, I am grateful to publisher Tod Thilleman and his team at Spuyten Duyvil, the most easy going collaborators I've ever had, for the production of the beautiful object you hold in your hands. Much the same can be said about my remarkable son, Joshua Salcman, who has designed the covers of nearly all my poetry collections and chapbooks.

The difficulties of being the spouse of a poet cannot be overimagined; the existence of this book is unthinkable without the love and support of Ilene Salcman, my brilliant wife.

Acknowledgments for the New Poems

The author gratefully acknowledges the editors of the following magazines in which the poems first appeared, sometimes in slightly altered fashion:

American Journal of Poetry: A Memory of Malaga & Blown Up

Arts & Letters: Visiting My Father in His Final Illness; Event Horizon; John Updike's Trash & Seven or Eight Reflections on Erik Satie

Barrow Street Review: A Poem Called Winter & Correspondence: Deep Yellow-Green

Blood and Thunder: In the Morgue

Burningword Literary Review: Walking the Edge of Death

The Café Review: The Empty House

The Cape Rock Review: Epiphany & Reversal

The Carolina Quarterly: How the Professor Rose

Clarion: The Best We've Ever Had

Cobalt Review: Summer Conference with D.D.

Common Ground Review: Getting Older

Concho River Review: Sake

Courtship of Winds: Three Days in Germany

Del Sol Review: Mannequins

Doubly Mad: First We Name You & A Song for Two Mothers

Ekphrastic Review: Muscles on the Muscle Man

Evening Street Review: The Good Tourist; Baltimore's East Side & The Hours

Free State Review: Because & The Burned Field

Gargoyle: Yesterday's News

Grey Sparrow: Rockefeller's Gift; Prayer for the Plague Year & 12 Reflections on Francis Picabia

The Healing Muse: Wounds

I-70 Review: The Cleft Chin

Journal of the American Medical Association: Lies Before Retirement

Lalitamba: Surrealism Comes with Age

LIPS: The Boys in the Office

Loch Raven Review: Pictures on a Trembling Wall & His Name Meant Light

Mad Poets Society: Insistence

Pangyrus: Intensive Care

Passager: No Translations for Love

Paterson Literary Review: His Tongue & Unreliable Narrator

Poet Lore: Every Picture But One

Poetry East: Poem to a Cane Placed Upside Down

Rat's Ass Review: White Space

Saranac Review: Self-Portrait as Serf

Sincerely Magazine: Old Fish

Slab: Social Distance in the City

Solstice: By the Way, What Time is It in Prague Milena?

South Florida Poetry Journal: Clement Greenberg Living in My Head Rent Free

Spank the Carp: Blind Spot

Stonecoast: Heard in a Museum: John Cage

Verse-Virtual: The Knife Thrower

"The Muscles on the Muscle Man" was reprinted in *Imagining Vesalius*, Rich Ratzan (editor), University of California San Francisco, Medical Humanities Division, 2020

"Rockefeller's Gift" was reprinted in *Catch the Moon*, Diane Smith & Natalie Schriefer (editors), 12th Anniversary Issue of *Grey Sparrow*, Grey Sparrow Press, St. Paul, 2020

NOTES FOR THE NEW POEMS in NECESSARY SPEECH

I

p. 7- Kafka's love letters to Milena Jesenská (1896-1944) have been collected; journalist, writer, editor, and translator, she died in the Ravensbrück concentration camp.

p. 12- After the Red Sea parts in the Torah, Miriam gathers the women in a circle of dance, song and instrumental rejoicing; Exodus: (Beshalach) 15:20-21.

p. 14- At the time of the "gift," Nelson Rockefeller (1908-1978) was Governor of New York; he was a major educational force and supporter of modern art.

p. 16- Henri Poincaré (1854-1912): French mathematician and polymath who almost discovered relativity before Einstein; wrote the best essay on mathematical creativity.

p. 20- Madame Defarge: a main fictional villain in *A Tale of Two Cities* who sat and knitted at the guillotine as the heads rolled off in the French Revolution.

II- Plague Poems & The Hours

p. 27- Bernard Rieux is the doctor/narrator in *The Plague* (1947), the frighteningly prophetic novel by Albert Camus.

p. 30- Wuhan is the name of the Chinese city where the 2020 plague began.

p. 32- Johannes Vermeer (1632-1675): almost all of his 34 extant paintings are about intimate interior subjects; one of the supreme artists of the Dutch Golden Age.

p. 33- Yehuda Amichai (1924-2000): perhaps the best poet in Modern Hebrew and the finest in that language since Judah Halevi (c.1075-1141) in Spain's Golden Age.

III

p. 52- Picasso was born in Málaga, a port city on Spain's Costa del Sol; father José Ruiz y Blasco, like Leopold Mozart, gave up art when his child outdid him.

p. 53- Clement Greenberg (1909-1994): America's most influential art critic; a pariah in the 1970s art world for strict advocacy of formalist criteria in judging artworks.

p. 55- Jack Whitten (1939-2018): important African-American abstract painter, sculptor and raconteur, invented many novel techniques for using acrylic paint.

p. 57- Guyanese-born Frank Bowling (1934), is the first Afro-Caribbean artist to be knighted; studios overlook the Hudson and the Thames. United the styles of Abstract-Expressionism and Color Field painting; see cover of *Shades & Graces*.

p. 58- Leon Polk Smith (1906-1996): born to indigenous parents in the Oklahoma Territory, pioneer of hard-edge abstract painting; revived the shaped canvas.

p. 59- Thomas Lux (1946-2017): remarkable poet, teacher and feisty baseball player at Sarah Lawrence College; early winner of the Kingsley Tufts Poetry Award.

p. 61- Deborah Digges (1950-2009): renowned poet, memoirist and teacher who ended her life in a fall; also won the Kingsley Tufts Poetry Award.

p. 63- Francis Picabia (1879-1953): early abstract painter of great wit, helped found the Dada art movement, turned to figuration, grandfather of Pop Art, and inventor of the 1980s.

p. 63- Max Reger (1879-1916): semi-famous composer and organist; acrimonious relationship with critic Rudolf Louis who provoked him with a February 7, 1906 review.

p. 66- Henri Matisse (1869-1954): incomparable painter and sculptor, great early and late; founded Fauvism in 1905 and invented scissor-cut painted paper collages in old age.

p. 69- Walter Benjamin (1892-1940): influential philosopher and art critic, authored *Art in the Age of Mechanical Reproduction*; Holocaust victim.

IV

p. 73- The Event Horizon lies at the edge of Black Holes; first postulated by Einstein, the point at which all objects and light waves are sucked in and destroyed.

p. 75- Andreas Vesalius (1514-1564): anatomist and author of *De humani corporis fabrica* based on his dissections (Basel, 1543); the most famous and beautiful medical book ever written. See page 181 of Book II (Basel on-line edition).

p. 76- Philosopher René Descartes (1596-1650) thought the soul resided in the centrally located pineal gland, a very challenging place in the brain for a neurosurgeon to be.

p. 77- John Cage (1912-1992): major composer and leader of post-war avant-garde; advocate of chance in art, like 4'33", a timed but silent performance.

A NOTE ABOUT THE TEXT

With few exceptions, the New Poems in *Necessary Speech* date from 2015 to 2021; Acknowledgements to the magazines in which they first appeared and a few Notes about the New Poems can be found above. I began The Plague Poems in Section II on March 15, 2020 and have not finished with them; the date at the bottom of each poem included here refers to the date of its first draft. They and The Hours were completed during the pandemic.

The Selected Poems are taken from my four previous collections; poems appearing only in one of my four chapbooks (2003-2007) are not included. Each Selected Poem was reviewed for possible editorial revision; some underwent minor changes, a few major surgery. By and large the selected shorter poems are those I enjoy performing in public. In general the long poems are presented in full. The majority of Selected Poems come from my two earliest books, *The Clock Made of Confetti* (2007), nominated for The Poets' Prize, and *The Enemy of Good is Better* (2011), both published by Orchises Press in limited editions. They appear here at the courtesy of the publisher, Roger Lathbury. My third collection, *A Prague Spring, Before & After*, winner of the 2015 Sinclair Poetry Prize from Evening Street Press, was devoted to family history and the Shoah; it contained a number of poems about these subjects reprinted from the first two collections. In *Necessary Speech*, all such poems have been returned to the original volumes in which they first appeared. Neither Lynn Silverman's beautiful Prague photographs nor the book's concluding prose poem/essay about family history and the events of 1968, are reprinted here. The latter device somewhat occupies the same literary space in *A Prague Spring* as Lowell's prose section in *Life Studies*. The remainder of *A Prague Spring* appears courtesy of its publisher Barbara Bergmann. The ample selection of poems from my fourth and most recent collection, *Shades & Graces: New Poems* (Spuyten Duyvil 2020), inaugural winner of the Daniel Hoffman Legacy Book Prize, appears courtesy of the publisher, Tod Thilleman.

No poems from my youth (1963-1977) are here, though some were published in "little" magazines during that time. No poems were written for publication during a decade-long hiatus from poetry (1977-1986). My apprenticeship to Tom Lux, Dick Allen, and many others, began around 1998 as did the reappearance of my poems in magazines and books.

MICHAEL SALCMAN, poet, physician and art historian, was born in Pilsen, Czechoslovakia, came to the United States in 1949 and trained in neurosurgery at Columbia University. Formerly chair of neurosurgery at the University of Maryland and president of the Contemporary Museum in Baltimore, he is the author of six medical textbooks and eight previous collections of poems, including *The Clock Made of Confetti*, nominated for the Poets Prize, *The Enemy of Good is Better*, and *A Prague Spring, Before & After*, winner of the 2015 Sinclair Poetry Prize. He edited *Poetry in Medicine*, a standard anthology of classic and contemporary poems about doctors, patients, illness and healing. His poems appear in prominent journals including *Arts & Letters*, *The Café Review*, *Harvard Review*, *Hopkins Review*, *Hudson Review*, *New Letters*, *Notre Dame Review*, *Poet Lore* and *Raritan*. His previous collection, *Shades & Graces: New Poems*, was the inaugural winner of the Daniel Hoffman Legacy Book Prize in 2020.

Made in the USA
Coppell, TX
26 March 2022

75574411R00187